TRAILBLAZERS

TRAIL BLAZ ERS

FOLLOWING THE PATH OF OUR UNSUNG SISTERS

LORI BOYD

ISBN-10: 1941972829
ISBN-13: 978-1941972823

Library of Congress Control Number: 2015958501

Published by Start2Finish Books
PO Box 660675 #54705
Dallas, TX 75266-0675
www.start2finish.org

Printed in the United States of America

Unless otherwise noted, all Scripture quotations are from the *New King James Version*. Copyright © 1979, 1980, 1982 by Thomas Nelson, Inc. Used by permission. All rights reserved.

Cover Design: Josh Feit, Evangela.com

To my mom, Anita Belihar

the strongest woman I know and my own personal trailblazer

TRAILBLAZERS

They were influential; they were obedient; they were
leaders used by God to accomplish great things. They
forged a path by faith and were remembered in His
Holy Word, yet their stories are often untold. They were
trailblazers!

ACKNOWLEDGEMENTS

In recent years I have been blessed with opportunities to partner my lifelong love for writing with my abiding love for God's Word, and I am grateful. *Trailblazers* is my first Bible study to be published, and it simply would not have happened without the help of some special people. From the bottom of my heart I would like to thank:

Sam, my husband, who is not only my best friend, but also my endless source of love and encouragement. God blessed me beyond measure when I became Sam's wife. I am a stronger person because he is walking with me to Heaven.

Evie, Kate, and Briggs, my children, who inspire me and keep me humble by showing me everyday what Scripture looks like in action. I love those three precious gifts.

My parents, Robert and Anita Belihar, who raised me in a Christian home and who taught me to cherish my womanhood and never question my worth; and my sisters, Jennifer Richardson and Julia Battles, whom I treasure as advisors, examples, and lifelong friends.

My friend, Tonja McRady, who has the heart of an encourager and has been such a support to me through this journey; and my friend Kristy Hinson, who motivates me, shares my love for writing, and truly helped make this book become a reality.

Michael Whitworth, who took *Trailblazers* from a saved file on my computer and made it into a published study guide for women everywhere; I am thankful to him for inspiring me to hit the "go" button!

Most importantly, I thank God my Father. I have learned that when

you pray for God to use you in His kingdom and then pray that
He will open doors, you better start getting yourself ready. He is
faithful! I humbly pray that God is glorified through this work and
that *Trailblazers* can be used as a tool to strengthen the spirits of
women and to further the Gospel of Jesus Christ.

PREFACE

I will always remember, as a child, hearing my mom tell Bible stories.
She made the men and women on the pages of God's Word come
alive, and I would listen with fascination as she described battles,
evil kings, dangerous journeys, and breathtaking miracles. I knew
that these stories were not like any other because they came from
the pages of God's Book: they were absolutely true.

Through those stories, my mom planted in my heart an enduring
love for the Bible. She made me feel like I knew Esther, that I
could sit down and talk to David, and that Jesus was as close to
me as the bear I held in my arms under the covers. Today, as a
grown woman, I look forward to the day that I will be able to meet
the Bible heroes and heroines who have taught me invaluable life
lessons and who have helped me to understand God's plan for His
people from the beginning.

The lessons that you will find in this book involve Old Testament
women whose true stories are often untold. I hope you will be
encouraged and that your faith will grow as you see the quality of
strength radiate through the lives of these remarkable women.
Some of their names you will recognize and others may be
completely unfamiliar to you, but I believe that studying the unique
characteristics of each of these women can help you on your

journey to becoming a stronger Christian serving in God's kingdom.

Our God values, loves, and cares for women. Throughout the Bible, we find many examples of how women involved themselves in the Lord's work, how they demonstrated their faith through obedience to God, how they influenced others as a result of their godly choices, and how God used them to accomplish His Will. They weren't inhibited by what they couldn't do; instead they changed lives because of what they could do.

Today, God needs women to do the same!

Whether it's teaching the Bible to a small child or to a room full of women, whether it's lifting some one up in prayer or sharing the Gospel in a personal Bible study, whether it's writing a note of encouragement or curriculum for Bible classes, the opportunities for women to work in the church are abundant and meaningful. The church needs Christian women who are teachers, speakers, writers, organizers, visionaries, and missionaries who can lead other women and children in their walks with God and take the message of the Gospel to the world. When we recognize the important roles we have and humbly follow the guidelines found in the New Testament, we empower ourselves and our daughters to use the talents we've been given in harmony with God's perfect plan for the organization and sustainment of His church.

The purpose of *Trailblazers* is to motivate women to become stronger for the cause of Christ. The Bible tells us that we must be prepared not only to fight for our faith, but also to defend it. This study will help women find the strength to do both.

AS YOU BEGIN...

I have prayed that those who embark on this journey with *Trailblazers* will be touched by the stories of these admirable women and inspired by their examples as I have been. I also encourage you to pray. Daily ask God to help you, to guide you, and to use you according to His Will. It is my hope that with each chapter you will grow in your faith, and by the end of the study, you will find that you indeed have the strength that it takes to "walk the trail!"

TIPS FOR USING THIS BOOK

ICONS

This journal icon appears next to the "field notes" entry at the beginning of each chapter. These are personal thoughts of mine "from the trail" that relate to the strength-building characteristics discussed throughout that chapter.

The "summit statement" is found next to this icon and summarizes the highest point of "The True Story". These sentences give a quick glimpse at the strength portrayed by the woman, or women, whose account is featured in that chapter.

These "two boots" give additional facts throughout the text in order to provide greater insight or meaning to the events taking place. These facts can be considered information... to boot!

By the flames, you will find suggestions for activities, acronyms to remember, inspiring quotes, songs, poems, or other motivating tid-bits. They are included in the chapter to help get you "fired up"!

When you see the tent, get ready to go camping! Next to this icon there are recommendations for further study—spiritual places to "camp out." You can spend time on these as you come to them, or return to them later in personal devotion.

The compass icon is found in a box at the end of every chapter. Next to the compass is a Scripture of strength that reinforces an aspect of the woman's account. It's a verse to take with you through the week to help keep you "on the right track"!

TRAILHEAD

Beneath the "Trailhead" you will read a brief summary of the events leading up to the Trailblazer's account—a starting point, if you will. Bible history is important to know, not only for the perspective that it lends to the accounts in this study, but for Christians to gain a better understanding of God's love for us and His plan for our salvation.

STRENGTH TRAINING TIPS

Under this heading is the application portion of each lesson located at the end of the chapter. For every woman in the study, there are four suggestions for developing the qualities of strength portrayed in her story. I've called these "Strength Training Tips" because this is where we put in the work! These tips can be reviewed individually or discussed in groups. We read the stories, discover the qualities that made these women strong, and then we begin our personal training by developing those qualities in our own lives. By doing this, we ready ourselves for walking the trail blazed by our sisters in Scripture.

◥ TRAILMARKERS

These are questions that accompany the lesson. They can be used in a personal study to review what was learned in the chapter or they can be used in a group setting to be filled out while the lesson is being presented.

STUDY SUGGESTIONS

Open Bible study – I would advise that when you begin each chapter of this study, you open your Bible to the text that goes along with the lesson. There are references to the text throughout the chapter and the lessons will be most effective if those Scriptures are read as they are encountered.

Individual study vs. group study – Trailblazers can be used as a personal Bible study or in a group setting, such as a devotional or Bible class. If you use the study in a group setting, I would suggest that you prepare by reviewing "The True Story" then share the account with the class without reading directly from the book. This is so much more engaging! As you retell the account, you can stop to discuss the questions I have included within the chapter and have the group turn in their Bibles to the Scripture references. You can read direct quotes from the lesson text for emphasis and include the "two boots" for extra information and discussion.

Involve group members in the application portion of the lesson, which is under the heading "Strength Training Tips." This part of the study is important because this is where the accounts of the trailblazing women and the qualities they possessed are translated to our lives today. It is through practicing these "tips" in daily life that we increase our strength.

Finally, I recommend that you include scenarios and current events to enhance the modern-day relevance of each lesson. Allow your group to talk about how they would respond in certain situations involving moral issues or occasions when their faith might be tested. Take the qualities highlighted in each chapter and create scenarios around those qualities. For example, Puah and Shiphrah demonstrated strength through their fear of God and their confidence, so that scenario would describe a "real-life" situation where those qualities can be exercised. These scenarios and news stories can be added at the end of each chapter as a supplement to the lesson.

Let's get walking!

CHAPTER 1

OUR STRONG SISTERS

LESSON TEXT /// ROMANS 15:4

Christian women can be strengthened through studying the stories and characteristics of women in the Bible. Some of the lesser-known women of the Old Testament were among the most influential, and their legacies live on in Scripture so that we might learn from their great examples of faith. They were trailblazers!

TRAILHEAD

A trailblazer is defined as "a person who forges a trail for others to follow through unsettled country or wilderness." She creates a path through rugged terrain so that those who come behind her might clearly see the direction in which they should go.

- Imagine a woman with two young children standing on either side of her, a handful of her tunic clasped in their tiny fists. Picture her leaving her home in Egypt, where she and her husband have suffered at the hands of the Egyptians year after year, and setting out under the darkness of night into the wilderness and toward a promising future. She says a quiet prayer of thanks to God for saving their nation and for Moses who would lead them to freedom.

- Imagine an older woman, shuffling through the sand with a walking stick in her hand. She stops for a rest and is instantly surrounded by lively children; they are crawling on her lap, holding her walking stick, and grabbing her hands. "Tell us the story about how God gave you Samuel! Please, tell us!" and with a gentle laugh she gathers up her grandchildren and begins to share her favorite story once again.

- Imagine a girl who is just entering into womanhood, with dreams in her heart and excitement in her eyes. Picture her standing by the roadside hoping for a glimpse of the boy called David who defeated the Philistine giant. After hearing about how the young shepherd boy killed the mighty warrior, she fashioned her own sling and practices throwing stones down by the brook with her younger brothers. She prays every day that God will use her to accomplish great things, too.

From the period of Egyptian captivity, through the wilderness wandering, during the times of the judges and kings, we meet many women on the pages of the Old Testament who are a testimony to faith in action. Those women faced challenges, overcame obstacles, suffered and struggled... yet they persevered and accomplished great things! Above all else, they loved God and demonstrated that love through obedience to Him; just as we are expected to do today (John 14:15).

When women question their worth, or doubt their ability to be meaningful and active participants in the work of the church, they can find answers in the lives of the godly women of the Bible whose accounts were recorded by inspiration for our learning. We can read and study their accounts, then follow their footsteps along the path they blazed; and in doing that, we will find strength within ourselves to be used for God's glory.

THE TRUE STORY

DEFINING STRENGTH

The trailblazing women chosen for this study have unique characteristics that promote an inner, unshakeable strength. As Christian women today, when we emulate the characteristics of these strong women of the Bible, we become stronger ourselves.

This strength is not the quality marked by great physical power, but rather the strength that will help us serve God more effectively in His kingdom, the strength that will help us in the battles we fight as Christians, the strength that will help us make the right choices based on sound judgments in our daily lives. Consider these other definitions of *strong*:

- Having force of character, will, morality, or intelligence
- Capable of withstanding force or wear; solid, tough, or firm
- Not easily captured or defeated
- Not easily upset; resistant to harmful or unpleasant influences
- Having force of conviction or feeling; uncompromising

This world needs strong Christian women: women who passionately do the work of the Lord with a steadfast faith and an unwavering dedication to the authority of God's Word.

DISCOVERING THE SOURCE

Our Old Testament sisters turned to God in faith to help them through trials, to guide their choices, to handle conflict, to pursue justice, and to withstand evil. They were strengthened through their dependence on God, their trust in His Will, and their belief in His Providential care.

Throughout the Bible, we find examples of how God demonstrated time and time again that through His power, His people would be made strong!

After Moses led the children of Israel out of Egypt, Pharaoh's heart was hardened once again, and he ordered their pursuit. When the Israelites reached the Red Sea, they looked back to see the Egyptian army marching toward them, and they panicked! Then God caused the waters of the Red Sea to divide so that Moses and the children of Israel could walk across on dry land. Standing on the other side, they watched as the waters came crashing down over the Egyptian army and their chariots, so that not one of them remained (Exodus 14).

Moses and the children of Israel sang these words of praise to the Lord:

*"**The Lord is my strength** and song, and He has become my salvation; He is my God and I will praise Him; my father's God and I will exalt Him"* (Exodus 15:2, emp. added).

The book of Psalms is abounding with references to our awesome and mighty God. David continually relied on his Heavenly Father to be the source of his strength. Spend some time reading the following psalms: 3, 8, 18, 23, 27, 28, 31, 55, 71, 86, 91, and 121. There are many others that can be added to this list, as well. Turn to these Scriptures when you are feeling troubled or when hope seems lost.

After declaring judgment on the kingdom of Judah because of their sin, the prophet Isaiah spoke these words of hope from God:

*"Fear not for I am with you; be not dismayed, for I am your God. **I will strengthen you**, yes, I will help you, I will uphold you with My righteous right hand"* (Isaiah 41:10, emp. added).

Paul wrote his last letter from a prison in Rome. He knew he would die for the cause of Christ. Many had deserted him in fear for their own lives, and he wrote these words to Timothy:

*"**But the Lord stood with me and strengthened me**, so that the message might be preached fully through me, and that all the Gentiles might hear. And I was also delivered out of the mouth of the lion"* (2 Timothy 4:17, emp. added).

One method of execution for first-century Christians was to place the person in an arena with lions. It is believed by some historians that Paul may have been describing an actual experience similar to Daniel in the lion's den. We cannot be sure, but it is an intriguing possibility.

Paul found strength in the Lord! He declared to the church at Philippi, *"I can do all things **through Christ who strengthens me**"* (Philippians 4:13, emp. added).

He encouraged the believers in Ephesus saying, *"Finally, my brethren, **be strong in the Lord and in the power of His might**"* (Ephesians 6:10, emp. added).

In his first letter, Peter addressed Christians about suffering for the cause of Christ and inspired them to be courageous in the face of persecution. In 1 Peter 5:10 (emp. added), Peter wrote:

*"But may the God of all grace, who called us to His eternal glory by Christ Jesus, after you have suffered a while, perfect, establish, **strengthen**, and settle you."*

The Bible tells us that we find strength in God!

DETERMINING THE PATH

As the Israelites began their journey out of Egypt and to the Promised Land, God led them in a pillar of cloud by day and a pillar of fire by night (Exodus 13:22). There was no smooth trail to follow; they had to maneuver over the rocky terrain, step around obstacles, and trudge through valleys, but always under the direction of their Heavenly Father. God, showing His grace, provided a way to lead His people to Canaan.

When the kingdom of Judah had wandered away from God, He called on them to "walk" in the "old paths," that is, return to following His commands, so "it would be well with them," and so they might "find rest in their souls" (Jeremiah 6:16 and 7:23). We have the same assurance today when we walk in the path of God's commandments. We can identify that path by reading and studying the Bible. In Psalm 119:105, David wrote, *"Your word is a lamp unto my feet and a light to my path."* The Word of God now serves as our "cloud by day and fire by night," and we can be sure of our direction when we follow its teaching.

The women we will study in the upcoming chapters walked a path according to God's Will and are remembered in Scripture for their obedient faith. It took strength for them to overcome challenges along the way. It took strength for them to keep going when the future seemed hopeless. It took strength to stay on the path when they felt completely alone. I want to have that kind of strength!

We are living in difficult times. Our world seems to be slipping further into darkness, and the threat of persecution is real for Christians. We must not give up! We can follow in the steps of our trailblazing sisters and learn from the characteristics that made them strong. When we apply those characteristics to our own lives, we can find the strength we need to remain steadfast on the path that will ultimately lead us to the Promised Land.

⬧ STRENGTH TRAINING TIPS

1.   **Define your source of strength**

Strength can come from a variety of sources. We are strengthened by our families and by our friends. We are strengthened by our successes, our education, and our careers. We are strengthened by physical and even financial accomplishments.

These can be positive sources of strength, but in what ways might they be inconsistent or variable? _____

_____

_____

Read Jeremiah 17:5-6. What does God tell us in these

verses? _____

_____

On what source of strength can you always depend? (Jeremiah 17:7) _____

_____

What characteristics does God possess that make Him the perfect source for strength? _____

2. **Search your heart**

Before meeting some of our trailblazing sisters, take a moment to look within yourself and evaluate your life at this very moment.

Where are you in your personal walk with God? _____

_____

_____

In what aspects of your spiritual life do you need to be stronger? _____

_____

What characteristics of strength do you already possess and how are you using them in your daily Christian walk? _

_____

_____

What have you experienced in your life recently that might be testing your faith? _____

_____

_____

_____

3. **Consider the strong women in your life**

In your personal life, who comes to mind when you think of strong Christian women? You know who they are!

They are those women you have encountered throughout your life whom you admire for their examples of faith, pictures of godliness, and wellsprings of wisdom.

What is it about those women that qualify them in your mind as being "strong"? _____

_____

_____

Do you notice any common characteristics within that group of women? _____

_____

_____

Write a note to a strong woman you know. Thank her for her example and mention specifically how she encourages you in your own faith. Pick someone right now in your mind....and do this today! She deserves to know that she is someone's heroine!

4.   Pray, study and trust

In order to grow in strength as Christian women, we must incorporate these three things into our daily lives:

WE PRAY that God will strengthen us (Isaiah 40:29) – Are you daily talking to God in prayer? (1 Thessalonians 5:17)

WE STUDY the Bible to increase our faith (Romans 10:17) – How often are you searching the Scriptures? (Acts 17:11)

WE TRUST in God to give us the help we need (Psalm 28:7) – Do you believe that God will take care of you?

(Jeremiah 29:11)

How will daily incorporating **prayer** in your life help you become a stronger Christian? _____

_____

_____

How will daily **Bible study** help you grow in strength? _____

_____

_____

How will demonstrating **trust** in God everyday make you stronger? _____

_____

_____

For whatever things were written before were written for our learning, that we through the patience and comfort of the Scriptures might have hope." Romans 15:4

◣ TRAILMARKERS

1. What is the definition of a *trailblazer*? _____

_____

2. In what way were faithful women of the Old Testament "trailblazers" for Christian women today? _____

_____

3. The women you will meet in this study loved God. According to the Bible, how do we demonstrate our love for God? (John 14:15) _____

_____

4. Being strong does not only mean having great physical power. Describe the type of strength we should strive to have as Christians. _____

_____

_____

5. Where did our Old Testament sisters find strength? _____

_____

6. Through what demonstration of God's power did the Israelites find strength after leaving the land of Egypt? ____

_____

7. What words of hope did Isaiah give the kingdom the Judah from the mouth of God? _____

_____

8. How did Paul tell Timothy and the church of Phillipi he received strength? _____

_____

_____

9. Paul encouraged the Ephesians by telling them to "be _____ in the Lord and in the _____ of his might" (Ephesians 6:10).

10. Where did Peter tell Christians in 1 Peter 5:10 they could find strength in the face of persecution? _____

_____

11. Where does the Bible tell us we can find strength? _____

_____

12. In Jeremiah 6:16, what does it mean to "walk in the old paths"? _____

_____

13. How can we know the path we should be walking as Christians? _____

_____

14. List the four strength training tips to implement as you begin this Bible study:

    1.

    2.

    3.

    4.

CHAPTER 2

PUAH AND SHIPHRAH

GOD-FEARING AND CONFIDENT

LESSON TEXT /// EXODUS 1:15-22

Only eight verses in the Bible are dedicated to the two women known as Puah and Shiphrah, but their actions would foil the evil plot of a powerful ruler and affect an entire nation.

"This is not what I believe at all!"

Those eight words tumbled out of an eight year old mouth from the back of a third grade classroom.

The students had started a new science unit that day, and the topic: "Evolution."

The first part of the lesson included a discussion about the earth's age. When her teacher announced the earth to be around four and a half billion years old, something did not sit well with one little girl on the last row. This was not what she knew to be true.

Her hand shot instinctively up into the air.

When her teacher called on her, my daughter gave that eight word rebuttal with all the conviction of a tender hearted child who loves God.

The teacher invited Evie to come up to her desk at the end of class and share her thoughts. After class, at her teacher's desk, Evie explained that God created the world and that the earth can only be thousands of years old, according to the Bible.

My child's teacher kindly looked into her eyes and said, "I believe in the Bible too, Evie, I just can't teach that in here."

I must realize that my children will be challenged on their beliefs, and it is my responsibility as a parent to make sure that when it happens they are ready with a logical, factual, biblical defense. I do not want to let them stand under fire and not have anything to say about why they can know that God is the Creator. I need to give them something! It is essential that they are able to say, "I believe that God created the world;" it is equally vital that they are able to continue on to say "and this is why..."

I cannot tell you how proud I was of Evie that day for declaring her disbelief in evolution. One small voice speaking out for the Truth! It leads me to wonder: what if Christians everywhere, when confronted with teaching that contradicts God's Word, collectively raised our hands and emphatically proclaimed, "This is not what we believe!"

◤ TRAILHEAD

In Egypt, a new pharaoh "who did not know Joseph" had come into power (Exodus 1:8). The Hebrew people, who had increased and prospered, were now reduced to the status of slaves because of their number and the threat of possible rebellion (vv. 9-11). In an effort to contain the Hebrew population, the new pharaoh called on two midwives to carry out a horrific order.

 *In Bible times, the primary role of the midwife was to assist a woman during childbirth. In v. 16 of the text, the Hebrew term for birth stool is* ovnayim *and literally means "two stones." It refers to the primitive form of a birth stool, which was simply two bricks, or stones, that a woman would sit on during labor.*

Take a few minutes to review the history of the Hebrew nation. How did God's people come to live in the land of Egypt? (Genesis 46:1-7) _____

_____

_____

⮚THE TRUE STORY

PHARAOH'S PLOT

The pharaoh of Egypt had a plan. The Hebrew population had to be controlled for the safety of his kingdom, and even though he had forced them into slavery, they continued to multiply and spread throughout the land. In fact, it seemed as if the more they were afflicted, the more their population grew. Something else had to be done! He sent for two Hebrew midwives, one named Shiphrah (from the Hebrew word "to beautify") and the other named Puah (from the Hebrew word meaning "to cry out").

The pharaoh of Egypt was the most powerful ruler in the world at this time in history. It was believed that his leadership was appointed by the gods.

Pharaoh gave Puah and Shiphrah an inconceivable and gruesome order. He instructed them that while they were helping the Hebrew women labor on the birth stool and found that a son had been born, then they should put the child to death, but the infant girls they would allow to live.

Stop for a minute and really think about this command Pharaoh gave. He wanted these two women to kill the baby boys that they were helping deliver. How did he expect for them to do this? The Bible doesn't say, but can you imagine what Pharaoh might have had in mind? It is horrific. Puah and Shiphrah found themselves in a frightening predicament. What Pharaoh asked of them was unthinkable, but disobeying him could result in the loss of their own lives.

PUAH AND SHIPHRAH'S RESPONSE

In v. 17 of the text, we read the response of Puah and Shiphrah to the pharaoh's order: "*But the midwives **feared God**, and did not do as the king of Egypt had commanded them, but let the boys live.*"

The Hebrew word for fear in this verse is *yare* (pronounced yaw-ray), which in this context carries the meaning to "revere, honor, or respect." The fear of God that Puah and Shiphrah demonstrated was characterized by obedience, not only because they were aware of God's judgment on sin, but also because they revered, honored, and respected Him. They refused to carry out the murderous request of the pharaoh, choosing instead to remain faithful to God regardless of the consequences they would certainly face. The women came up with their own plan!

Puah and Shiphrah continued their duties as midwives and let all of the Hebrew babies live. Pharaoh must have discovered their rebellion because v. 18 tells us that he sent for the women and asked them the question, *"Why have you done this thing and let the boys live?"*

Here is where Puah and Shiphrah's plan came into action. They **confidently** stood before Pharaoh and explained to him that Hebrew women, unlike Egyptian women, were vigorous and would already have given birth by the time the midwives arrived. At that point it was impossible to take the lives of the infant males who, by then, were safely resting in the arms of the mother. This explanation seemed to satisfy Pharaoh, who released them, and began working right away on another scheme to control the growth of the Hebrew nation.

What new command, in v. 22, did Pharaoh issue to all of his people regarding the Hebrew people? _____

_____

_____

GOD'S RESPONSE

Puah and Shiphrah were blessed because they feared God! The Bible says, "God was good to them" and that He "established households for them." In other words, He blessed them with large families, an indication of wealth and social status in those times. The actions of these two women also resulted in the multiplying and strengthening of the entire Hebrew nation.

A three-month-old baby boy, born to a Hebrew woman and saved from Pharaoh's cruel death sentence, was placed in a basket and set among the reeds of the Nile River. He grew to become a leader of the Hebrew nation and ultimately led them out of Egyptian bondage. It is believed that he may have been one of the infants saved by the brave midwives, Puah and Shiphrah. What was the name of that child? _____ (Exodus 2:1-10)

STRENGTH TRAINING TIPS

1.   **Have courageous confidence in the face of fear**

We may not ever be in the situation that Puah and Shiphrah found themselves, but we can ask the question, "Would I have the confidence to stand up against someone as powerful as a pharaoh if I were being asked to do something against God's Word?" What if we removed the phrase "as powerful as a pharaoh" from that question? Do you have the confidence to defend your Christianity in front of **anyone**, including family, friends, and co-workers, even when you are afraid of the consequence? Do you have the courage to raise your hand high and say, "This is not what I believe!"

What situations might we find ourselves in today that would require us to face fear confidently? _____

_____

_____

What are some things you can do to help increase your confidence and overcome your fears? _____

_____

_____

Read 2 Timothy 2:10 and 1 Peter 5: 9-10. What reasons do Paul and Peter give us for enduring hardship and suffering? _____

_____

_____

2. **Fear of God leads to blessings**

The fear we have for God is in wonder and respect for His power and in reverence for His ability to save us eternally (Hebrews 12:28-29). We learn to fear God by becoming familiar with His divine nature, which can be accomplished through reading and studying His Word. Certainly, we should be afraid of God's judgment on sin (Luke 12:5, Hebrews 10:31) and the discipline He gives His children (Hebrews 12:5-11); but as Christians we also have the comfort of knowing that God loves those He disciplines (Hebrews 12:6) and that *nothing* can separate us from that love (Romans 8:38-39).

Puah and Shiphrah feared God and, as a result, He blessed them both. God promises the same for us! Read Psalm 115:13 and complete this verse: "He will _____ those who _____ the Lord, the small together with the great."

How does reading the Bible help us develop a powerful fear of God? _____

_____

_____

How do we demonstrate our fear of God? (Deuteronomy 10:12-13 and Ecclesiastes 12:13) _____

_____

_____

3. **Believers do what is right in God's eyes, not in the eyes of the world**

Puah and Shiphrah honored the moral law of God rather than the words of Pharaoh. Remaining faithful to God's Law is of the greatest importance still today. In Acts 5:29, Peter and the apostles answered the high priest when he confronted them about continuing to teach of Jesus throughout Jerusalem, even after they had been punished and commanded to stop.

What did Peter and the apostles tell the high priest? _____

_____

_____

_____

In what situations might we demonstrate this today? _____

_____

_____

We can be sure that standing up for God's Law will
not always be easy. What does Paul tell Timothy
in 2 Timothy 3:12? _____

_____

_____

But remember the promise of Romans 8:35-37! What can
we know from these verses? _____

_____

_____

4. **We gain strength, courage, and power through a bond
with our sisters in Christ**

What might have happened if Puah and Shiphrah were
not united in their stand against Pharaoh? If one chose
to carry out Pharaoh's order and the other did not, one
woman may have died and many Hebrew boys may have
been killed. However, these women were undivided! I can
see them in my mind crying together, planning together,
encouraging each other, and praying together as they acted
on their faith in God. It had to have been a comfort to
know that they were not alone in that terrible situation.
The same comfort is available to us when we create a
bond with our Christian sisters.

Why is it important to develop relationships with our
sisters in Christ? _____

_____

How is that bond created and what can you do to nurture it?

_____

_____

_____

Whether you are the giver or the receiver, what happens as a result of sisters helping sisters? _____

_____

_____

This week schedule a lunch, dinner, or coffee date with one of your sisters in Christ, and choose someone who is from a different generation. You can make it a girls night out and get a group together—just be sure to have a mix of younger women and older women. The bond of sisterhood is a blessing!

"We ought to obey God rather than man." Acts 5:29b

⊼TRAILMARKERS

1. Where are the eight verses found in the Bible that tell the account of Puah and Shiphrah? _____

_____

2. What is the meaning of the Hebrew name Puah? _____

_____

_____

3.   What is the meaning of the Hebrew name Shiphrah? _____

_____

4.   What does Exodus 1:8 tell us about the new pharaoh who
      arose in Egypt? _____

_____

5.   What was Pharaoh's concern with the Israelite nation? ___

_____

6.   What happened to the Israelites as a result of this fear? __

_____

_____

7.   What was the significance of a pharaoh's position at this
      time in history? _____

_____

8.   Who were Puah and Shiphrah? _____

_____

_____

9.   What was the role of the midwife? _____

_____

_____

10.   As the Israelite nation continued to grow, what evil plot did
      Pharaoh create to control their population? _____

_____

_____

11.   What was the response of Puah and Shiphrah to Pharaoh's
      order as described in Exodus 1:17? _____

_____

_____

12. What response did the women give Pharaoh when he questioned their disobedience? _____

_____

_____

_____

13. What was God's response to the midwives? _____

_____

_____

_____

14. As a result of their actions, what happened to the Israelite nation? _____

_____

_____

_____

15. Who was born to a Hebrew woman, then hidden for three months, and would later lead the Israelite nation out of Egyptian bondage? _____

16. How did Puah and Shiphrah demonstrate their fear of God?

_____

_____

_____

_____

17. How did they demonstrate their confidence? _____

_____

_____

_____

_____

_____

18. List four strength training tips we can learn from the account of Puah and Shiphrah:

    1.

    2.

    3.

    4.

CHAPTER 3

MAHLAH, NOAH, HOGL'AH, MILCAH, AND TIRZAH

JUST AND REASONABLE

LESSON TEXT /// NUMBERS 27:1-11 AND 36:1-12

The five daughters of Zelophehad are remembered for their pursuit of justice in the first recorded lawsuit concerning a woman's right to land ownership and their willingness to accept the conditions God placed on His ruling.

I was having a bad hair day—plain and simple. I stood in front of the mirror trying to tame the blonde mop sitting on top of my head, which clearly had a mind of its own that morning. With an exasperated sigh I dropped my brush onto the counter, turned to my daughter Kate, and asked, "How does my hair look?"

With the sweetest smile she answered softly, "It's beautiful..."

My heart melted. "Thank you, Kate, that is just..."

Then before I could say another word, she added, "...even when it's ugly."

"Beautiful even when it's ugly." Hmmm. I wasn't quite sure how to take that one. It was an honest answer: sincerely, lovingly, and brutally honest.

At first, my feelings were hurt because I couldn't get past the word "ugly." But looking down at the face of my four year old it was obvious that she didn't intend to be mean. Her big blue eyes were looking up at me with admiration and love. I turned to face our reflections in the mirror, standing side by side in the bathroom. Me, in my old worn out bathrobe, sleepy-up-all-night eyes, a crazy mess of hair; and next to me, my daughter, who in spite of it all, thinks I'm beautiful.

I have to remind myself of this from time to time, especially on those days when I'm not my best self: days when I feel way, way less than beautiful—when I might not be very patient, I might lose my temper, I might let the kids watch movies all day, I might bring home Subway for lunch and order pizza for dinner.

There will be days when I might not be the best mother I can be, or the best wife I can be, or even the best Christian I can be; and I have to tell myself, when I have those "ugly" days, that I am still beautiful in the eyes of my children...my husband...and my Heavenly Father. Then I have to forgive myself and go back to being awesome (or really trying to be awesome) the next day.

Love sees beauty in disheveled hair, in tears, in mistakes, in burned broccoli, in a few stubborn pounds, in every display of inevitable *imperfection. God demonstrated that kind of love to the greatest degree when He sent His Son to die for us, while we were still sinners (Romans 5:8). How comforting and humbling it is to know that God looks past the ugly and sees something beautiful and someone worth saving when He looks at me!*

◣TRAILHEAD

God saved His people from Egyptian captivity through the leadership of His servant Moses, and the children of Israel had been wandering in the wilderness for forty years. At this time, they were preparing to enter into the Promised Land. Moses has been instructed by God to take a second census of the people.

The journey from Egypt to Canaan should not have taken 40 years! The constant complaining, unfaithfulness, and disobedience of the Israelite nation angered God and prevented a more timely passage into Canaan.

What specific event resulted in God requiring 40 years of wandering before the Israelites could enter the Promised Land? (Numbers 14:33-34) _____

_____

_____

It was only an eleven day journey from Horeb (also called Mount Sinai, where Moses received the Ten Commandments) to Kadesh-barnea (on the border of Canaan) according to Deuteronomy 1:2. The Israelites could have crossed into Canaan much sooner if they had simply trusted in God!

⧴ THE TRUE STORY

THE CENSUS

The Israelites gathered in the plains of Moab by the Jordan opposite of Jericho as the time for claiming the Land of Promise was at hand. God spoke to Moses and the high priest Eleazar and instructed them to take a census of the Israelite men, by tribe, including those twenty years of age and older. There were two specific reasons for the census. First, Moses could determine the number of individuals who were able to go to war for Israel because there would be much fighting once the Israelites crossed the Jordan River (Numbers 26:1-2). The second reason for the census was to prepare for the division of land in Canaan according to tribes. Larger families would receive a greater inheritance and smaller families, a lesser inheritance (Numbers 33:54).

What was the total number of men counted? (Numbers 26:51)

_____

_____

This is the second census taken by Moses recorded in the book of Numbers. The first census (chapter 1), counted in the Wilderness of Sinai, included the first generation of Israelites who left Egypt. Now, after 40 years of wandering and true to God's promise that none of that generation would enter the Promised Land except for Joshua and Caleb, a new census was being taken. This would be the second generation...plus two! (Numbers 26:63-65)

THE DILEMMA

Land ownership in Canaan would be divided by tribe and then divided among the families within the tribe. The head of every family would receive an allotment of land. However, only the men were counted in the census, and this created a problem within the tribe of Manasseh. In Numbers 26:33 we discover the issue, *"Now Zelophehad the son of Hepher had no sons, but only daughters; and the names of the daughters of Zelophehad were Mahlah, Noah, Hoglah, Milcah, and Tirzah."* Zelophed had died in the wilderness leaving only his unmarried daughters. If they did not speak up, their father's descendants would not receive an allotment of land...Zelophehad's name would disappear! With no father, no brothers, no husbands, and no in-laws, the five daughters of Zelophehad had no rights to land ownership!

JUSTICE PURSUED

Mahlah, Noah, Hoglah, Milcah, and Tirzah sought justice! They stood before Moses, Eleazar, and all of the leaders of the people, at the doorway of the tabernacle of meeting.

The tabernacle of meeting was the place where judgments on legal matters were made. If someone sought the Lord's counsel, they would take it to Moses at the tabernacle of meeting, and Moses would inquire of the Lord (Exodus 33:7-10).

Together they presented their case, *"Our father died in the wilderness, yet he was not among the company of those who gathered themselves together against the Lord in the company of Korah; but he died in his own sin, and he had no sons. Why should the name of our father be withdrawn from among his family because he had no son? Give us a possession among our father's brothers"* (Numbers 27:3-4).

Moses brought their case before the Lord.

Korah, from the tribe of Levi, along with 250 other leaders among the Israelites, led a rebellion against Moses and Aaron. Korah and his followers accused Moses and Aaron of "exalting themselves above the assembly of the Lord". When the matter was presented to God, He caused the ground to open and swallow Korah, his household, and those who stood with him. The other 250 rebels were consumed with fire sent from the Lord (Numbers 16).

THE LORD'S FIRST JUDGMENT

The Lord spoke to Moses and told him that Zelophehad's daughters were right! He instructed Moses to give them a "hereditary possession" among their father's brothers and that their father's inheritance should be transferred to them as well (Numbers 27:6-7). In vv. 8-11, God further explained to Moses what should be done with an inheritance in other unique circumstances. At the conclusion of His response to Moses, God commanded that His ruling become a "statutory ordinance" to the sons of Israel. In other words, the inheritance guidelines set forth by God would be instituted as law.

THE OBJECTION

The biblical account of Zelophehad's daughters does not end in Numbers 27. There is more to this amazing true story! A few books later (Numbers 36:1-4), we find out what happened after God ruled in the daughters' favor....

The heads of the households from within the tribe of Manasseh had a major concern.

If women who inherited property married outside of the tribe, their inheritance would be absorbed into the tribes of their husbands. In other words, if Mahlah, Noah, Hoglah, Milcah, and Tirzah married men from another tribe, their inheritance, which included their land, would become the property of their husbands.

What could this mean for the future of the tribe of Manasseh? (Numbers 36:4) _____

_____

THE LORD'S SECOND JUDGMENT

The Lord spoke to Moses and told him that the men of Manasseh were right! He commanded that the daughters of Zelophehad marry whom they wished, but their husbands had to be chosen from within the tribe of Manasseh (Numbers 36:5-9). That would prevent the inheritance of one tribe from being transferred to another tribe.

THE DAUGHTER'S RESPONSE

"Just as the Lord had commanded Moses, so the daughters of Zelophehad did" (Numbers 36:10). Mahlah, Noah, Hoglah, Milcah, and Tirzah obeyed God. They understood the importance of land and wealth remaining within their father's tribe and were reasonable in accepting the condition God placed on the new inheritance law.

The Lord kept his promise to the daughters of Zelophehad. As Joshua divided the territory of Canaan among the tribes of Israel, Mahlah, Noah, Hoglah, Milcah, and Tirzah stood with the sons of Manasseh and received their inheritance in the Promised Land! (Joshua 17:17)

◢ STRENGTH TRAINING TIPS

1. **Stand up for what is right**

   Zelophehad's daughters believed they were being treated unfairly and they sought justice in the appropriate way. They stood up for what was right...and God listened!

   In 1920, after over seventy years of struggle, women were finally granted the right to vote when the 19th Amendment was ratified. Most southern states were against the Amendment, and the vote came down to the state of Tennessee where it passed by one vote in the Tennessee house. The deciding vote was cast by Representative Harry

Burn who carried a letter in his pocket from his mother encouraging him to vote for women's suffrage.

Whether it is a mother writing a letter to her son calling on him to make a good choice or a woman speaking out against a violation of God's moral law, taking a stand for what is right is important and honorable.

Psalm 7:11 tells us, *"God is a just judge, and God is angry with the wicked every day."* What can you learn from that verse about the nature of God? _____

_____

_____

Have you ever had to take a stand for something you knew to be right? How would you handle a situation in which you, or someone you love, are (is) being treated unjustly? _____

_____

_____

2.   **Handle conflict directly and respectfully**

Did you ever play "telephone" as a child? This is the game where everyone sits in a circle and one person whispers a sentence to the person on her left. That person whispers the sentence to the next person and the sentence is passed around the circle until it comes all the way back to the first person. She announces the sentence that is whispered in her ear and then tells everyone what the original sentence had been. It is hilarious to hear how much the sentence changes as it is shared from person to person.

Gossip works in the same way, but it's never a game, and

in the end, no one is laughing.

Mahlah, Noah, Hoglah, Milcah, and Tirzah took their issue directly to the person who could help. There is no indication that they vented their frustration to their friends or spoke in bitterness or anger about their situation to others. Instead, they took their concern directly to the person who could help.

What might be harmful in sharing information with people who are not directly involved in a personal conflict you are experiencing? _____

_____

_____

What does the Bible say about gossip? (Ephesians 4:29; 1 Thessalonians 4:11; Proverbs 21:23) _____

_____

_____

_____

3. **Understand God's Will for your role in His church**

There is a role for everyone in the Lord's Church! We all have talents that can be used to His glory and there is always a means of implementing those talents in accordance with God's Word. When it comes to roles that God has set in the church, remember that it is not a matter of whether you have the ability to serve in a specific role; it is a matter of eligibility!

When the men of Manasseh took their concern to God regarding the future of the tribe...God listened. He placed a condition on the law of inheritance, and the daughters of Zelophehad obeyed it. The new condition did not devalue the women, and it didn't compromise their right to landownership; rather, it was implemented as a means of preserving the tribe.

How does the account of Zelophehad's daughters, including their God given right to claim their inheritance and the condition He placed on that right, relate to women in the church today? _____

_____

_____

If God would protect the future of the tribe of Manasseh, how much more would He protect the future of His church! How does structure and order, including the roles He designed for men and women in worship, ensure the preservation of the church? _____

_____

_____

4.   **Realize your worth in the eyes of God**

Read Galatians 3:26-28. It is important to recognize the context of these verses. Paul was writing to the Galatians about the promise of faith in Jesus Christ that might be given to those who believe (v. 22). He was not removing the different roles in which we serve; rather he was explaining the equality of all people who have obeyed the Gospel in terms of their salvation, calling those who belong to Christ *"heirs according to the promise."* In terms of status, Christians are all the same in God's eyes, although our functions in His kingdom are different.

How does realizing your worth to God motivate you to serve to the very best of your ability in the ways He has specified in the New Testament? _____

_____

_____

God can look right through my outward mess and see me as beautiful because of His Son, Jesus Christ. Describe what Jesus did to make that possible. _____

_____

_____

As God sees the worth in me, so I should see the worth in others. Take some time this week to write ten notes. Begin the notes with "Dear friend," and close the notes with "Someone who cares about you." In each note, tell the anonymous reader how special they are and how much they are loved. Share your favorite Bible verse with them or your favorite worship song. Seal up the notes and take them to a local nursing home. Ask the staff to give the notes to the residents who rarely have visitors or who never receive mail. You will brighten someone's day by simply recognizing his or her worth!

"He is the Rock; His work is perfect; for all His ways are justice, a God of truth and without injustice; righteous and upright is He." Deuteronomy 32:4

◣ TRAILMARKERS

1. Where do you find the account of Zelophehad's daughters in the Bible? _____

   _____

2. How many years did the Israelites spend wandering in the wilderness? _____

   _____

3. According to Deuteronomy 1:2, how long was the journey from Horeb (Mount Sinai) to Kadesh-barnea (on the border of Canaan)? _____

4. What was happening with the children of Israel at this time in history? _____

   _____

5. What special task did God ask Moses to undertake? ____

   _____

   _____

6. What were two reasons for performing this task?

   1.

   2.

7. Who was Zelophehad? _____

   _____

8. To what tribe did he belong? _____

9. How many children did he have? _____

10. What were the names of his daughters? _____

11. What injustice did Zelophehad's daughters face? _____

_____

12. What did they decide to do? _____

_____

13. What was Moses' response? _____

_____

14. What was God's response? _____

_____

15. What concern did the tribe of Manasseh have about the inheritance ruling? _____

_____

_____

16. What was God's judgment regarding that concern? _____

_____

_____

17. What was the response of Mahlah, Noah, Hoglah, Milcah, and Tirzah? _____

_____

18. What strength training tips can we learn from the account of Zelophehad's daughters?

   1.

   2.

3.

4.

CHAPTER 4

DEBORAH

INSPIRING AND BRAVE

LESSON TEXT /// JUDGES 4:1-16 AND JUDGES 5

Deborah served as a leader, a prophetess, and a judge who inspired loyalty among her people; she convinced an entire nation to take an extraordinary risk and believe in their ability to succeed.

The world bombards us with images of abuse, hatred, and evil. I find myself having to field questions from my children that I don't want to answer:

"Why can't we talk to strangers?"

"What does the devil look like?"

And most recently, "Why would that man shoot all of those people?"

Looking into the eyes of my children as I feebly try to explain the concept of "sin," I can't help but imagine the devil getting a kick out of the whole exchange. Quite honestly, he's getting on my nerves. The sadness is starting to melt away and what's left is a seething anger, not with my children for asking the questions, but rather with the evil forces that are incessantly striving to win them over. This mom is not going to let that happen, or at least I'm ready to put up a fight.

As Christians, we know 1 Peter 3:15, maybe not by memory but certainly by concept: "But in your hearts honor Christ the Lord as holy, always being prepared to make a defense to anyone who asks you for a reason for the hope that is in you; yet do it with gentleness and respect." Simply stated, always be ready to defend your faith. This verse is served up quite often when we talk about our responsibility as Christians in the world, and rightfully so!

I wonder if we could start adding a whopping spoonful of Jude 3, on the side? Jude writes, "Beloved, although I was very eager to write to you about our common salvation, I found it necessary to write appealing to you to contend for the faith that was once for all delivered to the saints." Here, Jude isn't calling on his readers to "defend" the faith; he is calling on them to "contend" for it! Consider this definition of the word "contend": "to engage in a competition or campaign in order to win or achieve something." Yes, we need to stand ready to defend our faith, but we also need to be actively competing for it! We need to put some offensive strategy into this battle we're fighting against the devil.

I'm determined to put a little Captain America into my battle plan! He uses his shield to protect him from his enemies, but he also handles it like a weapon and can take down the bad guys before they have a chance to attack. We have a shield too—a shield of faith (Ephesians 6:16), and I challenge us, as Christians, to use our shield in this battle of "good vs. evil," no holds barred. Let's not be defenders only! Let's be initiators, challengers, warriors for the cause of Christ!

◣ TRAILHEAD

In around the year 1200 B.C., the Israelites had possessed the Promised Land, and 120 years had passed since the death of Joshua. Upon entrance into Canaan, they had failed to drive out all of the inhabitants of the land as God had commanded; as a result, God allowed the other nations within Canaan to become a constant struggle for the Israelites.

Furthermore, when the Israelites did evil in the sight of the Lord, He did not prevent them from being enslaved by their enemies. They continued to demonstrate their typical cycle of behavior: turn away from God, face oppression, cry for help, and receive deliverance. God always heard their cry.

During that time, who did the Lord raise up to deliver His people? (Judges 2:16) _____

After Ehud, the second judge of Israel, died, God's people became unfaithful again and found themselves under the rule of Jabin the king of Canaan, who reigned in Hazor. He severely oppressed the Israelites for twenty years.

The Hebrew name for the book of Judges is Shophetim, which is translated "judges, rulers, deliverers, or saviors." *It was most likely written by Samuel, the final judge of Israel.*

✒THE TRUE STORY

ISRAEL ENSLAVED...AGAIN

After 80 years of peace, the Israelites lost their faith in God once again. They *"did evil in the sight of the Lord"* (v. 1), and He allowed them to become captives under the harsh rule of Jabin the king of Canaan, and Sisera, the commander of the Canaanites' intimidating army. The Israelites suffered twenty years of hardship at the hands of those men and their people.

The Bible mentions that Jabin's army had 900 iron chariots and many troops (vv. 3, 7, 13, 15). The Israelites were no match for that military force! In Judges 5:8, Deborah tells about her nation's lack of weaponry, singing "not a shield or a spear was seen among forty thousand in Israel." They needed God!

The Israelites cried to the Lord. They realized their helpless state. Notice that they didn't call upon any of the pagan gods they had falsely worshipped. They knew that only the one true God had the power to save them!

A UNIQUE WOMAN

Prior to being sold into the hand of King Jabin, the Israelites had been judged by a man named, Ehud. It was after Ehud's death that the Israelites began to turn away from God. It seems that without a judge to keep them in line, the Israelites were easily influenced by their ungodly neighbors.

During the period of slavery under the Canaanites, God raised up another judge within the Israelite nation: a woman by the name of Deborah.

 There were a total of fifteen judges who provided leadership for the Israelites before the first king of Israel was anointed. Ehud was the second and Deborah was the fourth. A man named Shamgar is recognized as the third judge and is mentioned briefly in Judges 3:31. Read the verse and you'll see that he must have been quite a man!

(NOTE: An ox-goad is a long stick with a pointed end that is used to prod cattle)

Deborah was a unique judge, not only because she was a woman, but because she was also a prophetess. A prophetess was simply a female prophet. Prophets and prophetesses had a very important role.

In Hebrews 1:1, what does the inspired writer say concerning how God used prophets in the past? _____

_____

_____

What did the Lord say as He stretched out His hand and touched the prophet Jeremiah on the mouth (Jeremiah 1:9)? "_____

_____"

Like Jeremiah, Deborah relayed the words of the Lord to the Israelites. She sat under a palm tree in the country of Ephraim and the people came to her for help and guidance in solving their problems.

Notice how Deborah refers to herself in the second part of Judges 5:7:

"...Until I, Deborah, arose, arose a _____ in _____."

This term beautifully describes her relationship with the Israelites. As a mother leads, cares for, protects, and loves her children, so Deborah served God's people and delivered them from persecution.

Along with judging Israel and serving God as a prophetess, Deborah was also the wife of a man named Lapidoth. She must have had responsibilities in her marriage and to her husband as well. Deborah was a truly special woman with many hats to wear.

In Hebrew, the name Deborah means "bee," a particularly fitting name for a woman who worked hard for the Lord and, like sweet honey, her diligent service provided a fruitful harvest.

AN IMPORTANT MESSAGE

One day, Deborah sent for Barak, a military leader of the Israelite nation, and asked him about a special instruction that had come from the Lord. The Lord had commanded Barak to take ten thousand men from the tribes of Naphtali and Zebulun and confront Sisera, the leader of Jabin's army. Even though the Lord had promised that Sisera would be delivered into Barak's hand, Barak had failed to act and Deborah wanted to find out why. Barak may have been afraid or he may have doubted his ability to lead; whatever the case, he only agreed to fight Sisera's army on one condition.

In v. 8, what was the condition that Barak set in response to Deborah? _____

_____

_____

_____

_____

DEBORAH INSPIRES A MAN AND A NATION

The Israelite nation lived in fear of their oppressors, and in front of her stood Israel's military leader who lacked faith in his ability to lead a revolt against the Canaanites, despite the Lord's promise for victory. Deborah found herself in a precarious situation: One woman against Barak and an army of men who needed a gentle push. Barak needed encouragement. He needed reassurance from God's messenger that everything would be okay. Deborah, a woman, would inspire Barak and all of Israel to fight!

She answered Barak and said, "*I will surely go with you...,*" but went on to say that there would be no glory in the journey Barak was about to take because the Lord would allow Sisera to be delivered into the hand of woman.

One might think that the woman God was referring to was Deborah, but there is a very fascinating turn of events that will result in that distinction falling to another; a woman we will learn more about in the next chapter of this study who is referred to as "most blessed among women" (Judges 5:24).

Deborah went with Barak to Kedesh then on to Mount Tabor, as commanded by God, with ten thousand men from the tribes of Naphtali and Zebulun. In going with them, she served as a physical reminder of God's promise. They knew her to be their judge, and they knew her to be a prophetess; for those reasons, they knew without a doubt that God would deliver them as she rode alongside them toward the battle.

THE BATTLE CRY

The report came to Sisera that Barak the Israelite had recruited an army and assembled them on Mount Tabor. So Sisera gathered his 900 chariots of iron and the people of his army and stationed them at the River Kashon, just as the Lord had said it would happen. Then at the top of Mount Tabor, Deborah faced Barak, the leader of the Israelite army, and said, *"Up! For this is the day in which the Lord has delivered Sisera into your hand. Has not the Lord gone out before you?"*

So Barak went down from the mountain grossly outnumbered and at a significant military disadvantage, but brave Deborah had looked into his eyes and reminded him of the Lord's promise, and it gave him the courage to go.

People have wondered why Barak is mentioned in Hebrews 11:32 as an example of faith and Deborah's name is not listed. If you read vv. 32-34 of that chapter, you'll find that all of those named were men who, because of their faith, physically went into battle for God's people. There is nothing in Scripture that indicates Deborah actually fought; it would most likely have been prohibited because she was a woman. Remember, it wasn't until 2013 that women were given the right to fight on the front lines of battle in the United States! It was Barak's faith, strengthened by Deborah's actions, which motivated him to lead the Israelites in battle against the Canaanites. Her name not being found in Hebrews 11 has no bearing on the fact that she was a great leader and a faithful servant of the Lord!

STRENGTH TRAINING TIPS

1. **If you are going to be a "hat collector," be a Christian "hat collector"**

    Like most women today, Deborah collected hats. She wore the judge hat, the prophetess hat, the wife hat, and the mother-figure-to-an-entire-nation hat! She had duties to fulfill in each role and, at times, it might have been difficult for her to meet everyone's expectations.

    Read Colossians 3:17 and fill in the blanks: *"And whatever you do in _____ or _____, do all in the _____ of the _____, giving _____ to God the Father through Him."*

When we put Colossians 3:17 into practice, how does it affect our hat-wearing? _____

_____

_____

_____

_____

In what ways can we ensure that our Christianity comes first, regardless of the many responsibilities we have? ____

_____

_____

2.   **Never underestimate your ability to inspire others**

We can look to Deborah as a powerful example of how to be an inspiration to others. Notice the ways in which she inspired Barak:

- She reminded Barak of the Lord's promise of victory (Judges 4:6-7)

- She rode with him to battle (Judges 4:10)

- She celebrated his accomplishment (Judges 5:12)

We can do the same for those in our lives who need encouragement!

Remind others of God's promises, be there for them when they need you, and celebrate their victories—no matter how small.

What promises has God given that you can share with others to give them inspiration? (Here are just a few...

Philippians 4:19; Romans 8:28; 1 Corinthians 10:13; Mark 16:16; and 1 John 2:25) _____

_____

_____

3.   **Women are brave and can fight for the Lord**

Paul tells Timothy in 1 Timothy 6:12 to *"fight the good fight of faith,"* and in 2 Timothy 2:3-5, Paul writes that we must *"endure hardship as a good soldier of Jesus Christ"* and not *"entangle ourselves with the affairs of this life."* As Christians, we were all enlisted in God's army when He added us to His kingdom. The battle we are fighting is spiritual in nature, against Satan and his evil forces (Ephesians 6:11-12).

We can be brave in knowing that God is on our side and is fighting for us! (Deuteronomy 3:22; 31:8; Joshua 1:9; Jeremiah 1:8). We can also be brave in knowing that we will be victorious in the end (1 Corinthians 15:57)!

A spiritual battle requires the use of spiritual weapons (2 Corinthians 10:3-4) and God has given us the armor we need to withstand the devil's attacks (Ephesians 6:11-20).

How are you training to fight in your spiritual battles? _____

_____

_____

_____

How does knowing that God is fighting with you help you in your daily battles? _____

_____

_____

4.   **Women can be righteous leaders**

Women can provide leadership in a variety of ways that coincide with the guidelines given to us in the New Testament. We need strong Christian women who can influence and guide others in the Truth!

Keep in mind the righteous leadership of Lydia, Priscilla, Anna, Dorcas, Mary and Martha, Lois and Eunice, the woman who anointed the feet of Jesus, the Canaanite woman, and many others found on the pages of the New Testament who influenced others through their demonstrations of faith.

The description of the "Virtuous Woman" in Proverbs 31 gives a beautiful picture of righteous leadership.

Read Proverbs 31:10-31 and identify characteristics of leadership portrayed in the life of this godly woman. _____

_____

_____

Name another women in the Bible who demonstrated righteous leadership. _____

_____

What was it about her that made her a leader? _____

_____

_____

"Have I not commanded you? Be strong and of good courage; do not be afraid, nor be dismayed, for the Lord your God is with you wherever you go." Joshua 1:9

◤TRAILMARKERS

1. Where do we find the account of Deborah in the Bible? ___
    _____

2. How long has it been since Joshua's death? _____
    _____

3. The Israelites are currently under the rule of whom? _____
    _____

4. How long had the Israelites been under their current state
    of oppression? _____
    _____

5. How did Israel's army compare to that of their oppressors?
    _____
    _____

6. Who was the commander of the Canaanite army? _____
    _____

7. Who did God call to judge His people at this time? _____
    _____

8. Describe the roles in which Deborah served? _____
    _____

_____

9. Where did Deborah prophesy to her people? _____

_____

_____

10. What is the meaning of her name in Hebrew? _____

_____

11. Whom did she send for to question about leading the
    Israelites into battle and what was his occupation? _____

_____

12. What did Deborah ask him? _____

_____

13. What was his response? _____

_____

14. Why was he afraid? _____

_____

15. What would happen as a result of his fear? _____

_____

16. Why would Barak and his men feel more confident having
    Deborah accompany them on their way to the battle? _____

_____

_____

17. When Sisera was gathered at the River Kishon, what words
    did Deborah speak to Barak? _____

_____

_____

18. What lessons in strength training do we learn from the account of Deborah?

   1.

   2.

   3.

   4.

CHAPTER 5

JAEL
OPPORTUNISTIC AND RESOURCEFUL

LESSON TEXT /// JUDGES 4:17-24 AND JUDGES 5

Referred to as the "most blessed among women," Jael came face to face with an enemy far superior in physical strength; and in one defining moment, using what she had within her grasp, brought the Israelites' oppressive captivity under the Canaanites to a dramatic end.

I love Paul's letters. I learn something new every time I read one. I find it amazing that words written by a man hundreds of years ago to struggling churches can still teach and encourage a forty-something year-old mother of three sitting at a kitchen table in Murfreesboro, Tennessee. I am so thankful God gave us the Bible.

Before you delve into Colossians, keep in mind that Paul is in prison at the time he wrote this letter. That way, as he speaks about prayer, rejoicing in suffering, setting your mind on things above, forgiveness—you may gain greater appreciation for his perspective. It carries more power when a man in chains calls on you to let the peace of God rule in your heart and to be thankful. Wow—what an incredible example!

On this occasion of study, God, through Paul, taught me something about opportunity. I read Colossians 4:2-4, which says, "Continue earnestly in prayer, being vigilant in it with thanksgiving, meanwhile praying also for us, that God would open to us a door for the word, to speak the mystery of Christ, for which I am also in chains, that I may make it manifest, as I ought to speak."

I find that I pray frequently that God will help me to be a better Christian, wife, and mother; that He will help me to be a good example to people around me; and that He will help me to make good choices. I recognize the importance of asking for His help in all that I do, but I discovered something else important in Paul's statement to his brothers and sisters in Colosse. He asked them to pray that God "would open a door." He prayed for opportunity! His request was that God provide them with a situation where they might be able to speak to others about Christ. I can't remember ever specifically asking God to present me with an opportunity to tell someone about Jesus, but I will now, thanks to Paul's nearly 2000 year-old letter!

I believe asking for "open doors" in our personal prayers could be life changing. My only caution is, with the knowledge that "whatsoever you ask for in prayer, believing you might receive," we better be ready to enter those doors when they begin to open!

◤TRAILHEAD

Deborah, a judge and prophetess in Israel, had received word from the Lord that He was going to lead the Israelites to victory over their Canaanite oppressors. She inspired Barak, the military leader of the Israelites, to assemble ten thousand men and rise up against Sisera, the commander of the Canaanite army.

In Judges 4:11, a man named Heber the Kenite is mentioned. What does the verse tell us that Heber had just done? _____

_____

_____

The Kenites are first mentioned in the Bible in Genesis 15:19, as the Lord listed them among the inhabitants of Canaan whose land would become the inheritance of Abram. They were a nomadic tribe of metalworkers and coppersmiths.

_____

During the time of the Israelite captivity under the Canaanites, it is speculated that the Kenites may have provided the army of King Jabin, under the direction of Sisera, with their impressive iron chariots and weaponry.

_____

The Kenites had a friendly relationship with the Canaanite people; however, they also had a peaceful and deep-rooted connection with the Israelites. Jethro, the father-in-law of Moses, was a Kenite, and his descendants had accompanied the Israelites on part of their journey to Canaan. We read in Judges 1:16 that they departed after the conquest of Jericho (the City of Palms) and settled in the wilderness of Judah.

The relationship between the Kenites, the Israelites, and the Canaanites is important to understand, as the heroine of our story, Jael, has a unique link to each of those nations affording her the opportunity to be the right person, in the right place, at the right time.

⮑ THE TRUE STORY

THE BATTLE

After hearing the battle cry of Deborah, Barak marched down from Mount Tabor with ten thousand men following him to face Sisera and the Canaanite army. Sisera had assembled his chariots and all his people by the River Kishon. Details of what happened next can be found in Judges 5, the song sung by Deborah and Barak.

"Lord, when You went out from Seir, when you marched from the field of Edom, the earth trembled and the heavens poured, the clouds also poured water; the mountains gushed before the Lord, this Sinai, before the Lord God of Israel" (vv. 4-5).

"The torrent of Kishon swept them away, that ancient torrent, the torrent of Kishon. O my soul, march on in strength! Then the horses' hooves pounded. The galloping, galloping of his steeds" (vv. 21-22).

The Lord sent a great rain that caused the Kishon River to overflow its banks where Sisera's army was stationed! The waters swelled and the land along the river's path became a sea of mud. Sisera's army, along with its horses and chariots, became bogged down in the mire. According to Judges 5:21, some were swept away by the strong and fast moving waters of the Kishon, while others managed escape only to be pursued to Barak and the Israelite army.

74

How many of Sisera's army survived the battle? (Judges 4:16) ___

It is ironic that Baal, the main god worshipped by the Canaanites, was the god of sun and storms....yet, the Canaanites lost the battle because of heavy rains!

SISERA'S ATTEMPT TO RUN

When Sisera realized the fate of his army, he abandoned them, came down from his chariot, and ran away on foot. He fled to Zaanaim to the tent of a woman named Jael, who was the wife of Heber the Kenite.

In Hebrew, the name Jael means "mountain goat," a fitting name for a woman belonging to a nomadic tribe living near the mountains of Kedesh and who possessed characteristics that would help her survive harsh conditions!

What reason is given in Judges 4:17 as to why Sisera looked for refuge at Jael's tent? _____

Jael went out to meet Sisera, who must have been exhausted physically and emotionally from the battle and his escape, and she called him into her tent: "Turn aside, my lord, turn aside to me; do not fear."

At this time in history, it would have been common practice for a man to have more than one wife. Each wife would have her own tent that she would live in and maintain. When she had children, they would live there with her as well.

JAEL SEIZED THE MOMENT

Sisera entered the tent of Jael. He was afraid, knowing that Barak was in pursuit and that his life was in danger. Jael covered him with a rug and Sisera asked her for a little water to drink. An **opportunity** became clear to Jael and she seized it! She opened a jug and gave him a drink....but it was not water!

What did Jael give Sisera to drink? (Judges 4:19) _____

 Milk contains tryptophan, which helps in the production of serotonin and melatonin, chemicals that induce sleep.

Jael covered Sisera again. He gave her strict instructions to follow if anyone should come looking for him:

"Stand at the door of the tent and if any man comes and inquires of you, and says, 'Is there any man here?', you shall say 'No.'"

Then Sisera fell asleep.

Jael had to act quickly! There in her tent the commander of the

Canaanite army lay sleeping, and it was clear that someone was looking for him. What followed was one of the most graphically described murders in the Old Testament. Read the words recorded in Judges 5:

"She stretched her hand to the tent peg.
Her right hand to the workmen's hammer;
she pounded Sisera, she pierced his head,
she split and struck through his temple.
At her feet he sank, he fell;
where he sank, there he fell dead" (vv. 26-27).

Using a hammer and a tent peg used for securing the ropes of the tent, the resources she had immediately available to her, Jael killed Sisera by driving the peg deep into the side of his head.

 Here is a picture of ancient Roman iron tent pegs dated from around the 2nd or 3rd century A.D.

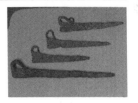

What was her motive? The Bible does not tell us, but we can consider the possibilities:

- She felt a loyalty to God and Israel
- She was concerned for her safety
- She had suffered under Sisera

Whatever her motive may have been, she saw an opportunity to protect herself and her family, she had resources available to her, and she took action.

It must have been known that it was Barak of the Israelites who pursued Sisera, because Jael ran from her tent to meet him and said, *"Come, I will show you the man whom you seek."*

When Barak entered the tent of Jael, he found Sisera dead with the tent peg in his temple. Imagine his shock at the sight! The words of Deborah must have echoed in his mind, *"...there will be no glory in the journey you are taking, for the Lord will sell Sisera into the hand of a woman."*

On that day, God subdued King Jabin of Canaan in the presence of the Israelites. They continued to grow stronger and stronger against King Jabin, which eventually led to his destruction.

What occurred in the land following the end of the Israelite oppression by the Canaanites and the deaths of King Jabin and Sisera? (Judges 5:31) _____

▰ STRENGTH TRAINING TIPS

1.   **"Redeem the time"**

In his letter to the Ephesians and again in his letter to the Colossians, Paul used a phrase that has become one of my favorites. He admonished those Christians to walk in wisdom, *"redeeming the time"* (Ephesians 5:15-16; Colossians 4:5). Some newer translations replace that phrase with *"making the most of every opportunity,"* however, the words *"redeeming the time"* reflect a deeper, more beautiful meaning in Paul's message.

The Greek word for *redeem* in those verses is *exagorazo*, meaning "to purchase out of." It is used on two other occasions by Paul to explain how Christ redeemed us, or "paid the price to remove us," from the old law (Galatians 3:13; 4:5). It could be described as "rescuing someone out of a bad situation."

The Greek word for *time* used there is *kairos*, and refers to an appointed or opportune time. It's the specific time to perform a task that will pass if action is not taken, for example, *"It is 'time' to go to Bible class."*

So then, why are we "purchasing appointed times" and from what are we saving them? Paul gives us the answer in Ephesians 5:16, *"because the days are evil."* Simply stated, we are rescuing opportunities from a sinful world.

We should seize opportunities to do good! Grab hold of moments that can make us stronger Christians! Walk through open doors to spread the Gospel! If **we** don't "redeem the time," the evil forces around us will.

In what way did Jael "redeem the time?" _____

_____

_____

_____

How are you "redeeming the time" in your life and making the most of opportunities that approach your tent? _____

_____

_____

Pray for an opportunity to share the Gospel with someone. God will open a door!

2. Use the resources that you have been given

In the 1948 Walt Disney movie *So Dear to My Heart*, the wise owl sings a song called *"It's Whatcha Do with Whatcha Got."* The idea is that everyone has something to offer. We've all been blessed with certain talents and abilities, and regardless of the amount we have, what matters is how we use them.

Take a few minutes this week to watch the "It's Whatcha Do with Whatcha Got" clip! You'll be humming that tune and thinking about all the big things you can do with just a little!

Jael belonged to a tribe of nomads and had immediate access to tools required for constructing and setting up tents. She had those resources available and when she needed them, she didn't hesitate to use them. Of course, Jael's situation was unique and we never use our resources to harm or threaten someone.

Ask yourself the questions: What resources do I have? What is within my reach that I can use to help further the cause the Christ? What is in **my** hand? _____

_____

_____

What are your special talents and abilities? How are you using them to glorify God and further His kingdom? _____

_____

_____

3. **You have strength that surpasses physical limitations**

Remember, the definitions of "strong" that we talked about back in the first chapter? One definition was "resistant to harmful or unpleasant influences." A strong woman will stand up against those things in life that can hurt her or weaken her faith. This strength comes from determination and conviction and is not measured by physical power. Some of the strongest women I know walk with a cane.

Jael defeated a warrior. While we may not ever have to confront a warrior, we do sometimes face situations or temptations that seem to overpower us. How do we find the strength to overcome those difficulties? _____

_____

_____

Our strength comes from God. It is a strength that is not inhibited by our physical bodies. It may not be demonstrated through outward displays of force, rather it is a quiet strength, characterized by confidence and faith, which provides us with the ability to fight the spiritual battles that are waged against us in this world.

How would you describe the strength that comes from

God? _____

_____

_____

4. **Keep your temple in good repair**

The focus of this study is inner strength, but the importance of taking care of our physical bodies should not be ignored.

"Or do you not know that your body is the temple of the Holy Spirit who is in you, whom you have from God, and you are not your own? For you were bought at a price; therefore glorify God in your body and in your spirit, which are God's" (1 Corinthians 6:19-20).

How can our bodies bring glory to God? We can improve our physical health so that we can better serve Him. When we take care of our bodies through exercise and good nutritional habits, we strengthen ourselves so that we can carry out the work of the Lord. We cannot neglect the temple of the Holy Spirit!

What steps are you taking to strengthen your physical body?

_____

_____

_____

How is taking care of our bodies an aspect of stewardship?

_____

_____

_____

Walking is one of the best forms of exercise, and whether it's through your neighborhood, along a nature trail, or around the perimeter of your house, taking time to walk for 20 minutes every day will make a difference in your health. Walking also provides the perfect opportunity to spend time with God in prayer. Start taking a daily "prayer walk" and see what happens!

"For God has not given us a spirit of fear, but of power, and of love, and of a sound mind." 2 Timothy 1:7

◤TRAILMARKERS

1. Where do we find the account of Jael in the Bible? _____

_____

2. Who were the Kenites? _____

_____

_____

3. What was the relationship of the Kenites to the Israelites?

_____

_____

4. Describe what happened in the battle between the Israelites, led by Barak, and the Canaanites, led by Sisera.

_____

_____

_____

5. To what city did Sisera run after his army was defeated? __
_____

6. Whose tent did Sisera approach? _____
_____

7. Who was she? _____
_____

8. What is the meaning of her name? _____
_____

9. Why did Sisera approach her tent? _____
_____

10. What did he ask of Jael? _____
_____
_____

11. What did Jael give Sisera to drink? _____
_____

12. What did Jael do once Sisera was asleep? _____
_____
_____
_____

13. Who was pursuing Sisera and was met by Jael outside of her tent? _____

14. What was the ultimate outcome of these events? _____
_____
_____

15. What motive does the Bible give for Jael's actions? _____
_____

What are some possibilities? _____

_____

_____

16.   What prophecy made by Deborah was fulfilled in the death
       of Sisera? (Read Judges 4:9). _____

       _____

       _____

17.   In what way was Jael opportunistic? _____

       _____

       _____

18.   In what way was she resourceful? _____

       _____

       _____

19.   What strength training tips can we learn from the account
       of Jael?

       1.

       2.

       3.

       4.

CHAPTER 6

JEPHTHAH'S DAUGHTER

SELFLESS AND SUBMISSIVE

LESSON TEXT /// JUDGES 11:29-40

We are never told her name in Scripture, but she is remembered for her unselfish response to an impulsive vow made by her father and her willingness to submit to a fate that she did not choose.

At the 2010 Wimbledon Championships, John Isner and Nicolas Mahut played the longest running match in tennis history. After 11 hours and 5 minutes, over a three day period, Isner won 70-68 in the fifth set after breaking Mahut's serve for only the second time all match. A backhand by Isner, straight down the line, ended the historical event. At the close of the second day of play, Isner was quoted as saying, "He's serving fantastic. I'm serving fantastic. That's really all there is to it." This match defined itself by the service of the two players. Their demonstration of skill in their ability to serve drew the attention of people all over the world.

Taking this idea of "fantastic serving," I find I can apply it to my own life in a more personal way. I consider, as a Christian, how I am called to serve. Jesus taught that true greatness could be found in serving others. In Matthew 20, He said to His disciples, "Whoever desires to be great among you, let him be your servant. And whoever desires to be first among you, let him be your slave–just as the Son of Man did not come to be served, but to serve, and to give His life a ransom for many." Jesus offered help and hope to the sick and sinner, He admonished His followers to feed and clothe those in need, He washed the feet of His dearest friends as an example of humility, and He suffered unimaginable pain as He died on a cross in the ultimate expression of love for man. Perfect service to others characterized His entire life on this earth, and in the end He brings victory to all those who believe and obey Him.

I am to be an imitator of Christ as Paul encouraged the Corinthians. What better way to display my likeness to Him then in my willingness to serve others through love? I heard something in a Sunday morning lesson many years ago: If I had been the only person in existence at the time Christ came to live on this earth–He still would have given His life for my salvation. He served me personally when he followed the will of His Father and chose to endure crucifixion at Calvary. I cannot think of a more powerful motivation to improve my service to others than that.

◤TRAILHEAD

Following the defeat of the Canaanites under the leadership of Deborah and Barak, Israel had rest in their land for forty years, but as was their normal pattern of behavior, they began to do evil and soon found themselves oppressed by the Midianites. That period of oppression lasted for seven years (Judges 6:1).

Who was chosen by God to deliver the children of Israel from the Midianites? (Judges 6:11-14) _____

_____

After Gideon's death, Abimelech attempted to appoint himself ruler over Israel, but failed horribly, and then two more judges arose to save God's people. After they died, Israel again did evil and was delivered by the Lord into the hands of the Philistines and the Ammonites.

How long did this period of oppression last? (Judges 10:8) _____

_____

When the Ammonites crossed over the Jordan to fight against the tribes of Judah, Benjamin and Ephraim, the Israelites began crying out to the Lord to the point that the Bible says, *"His soul could no longer endure the misery of Israel"* (Judges 10:16).

The Ammonites set up camp in Gilead, and the Israelites came together and camped in Mizpah. The leaders of Gilead began to ask the question and make the vow, *"Who is the man who will begin the fight against the people of Ammon? He shall be head over all the inhabitants of Gilead"* (Judges 10:17-18).

_____

 The tribe of Reuben, the tribe of Gad, and half the tribe of Manasseh were included in the territory of Gilead, which was located east of the Jordan River.

_____

➤ THE TRUE STORY

A MIGHTY MAN OF VALOR

Jephthah was a valiant warrior from the tribe of Manasseh, the son of a man named Gilead but also the son of a harlot. When Gilead married, he and his wife had sons who grew up and rejected Jephthah because he was the son of another woman. In fact, they told him that he would have no inheritance in his father's house.

 Jephthah's father's name was Gilead and his family also lived in the territory of Gilead...it can be a little confusing!

Jephthah ran away from his half-brothers and found a place to live in the land of Tob. While in Tob, other men, whom the Bible describes as "worthless," joined together with Jephthah and they would all go out raiding together.

 Jephthah's name in Hebrew means "He will open." In this story we will find that Jephthah "opened" his mouth quite a bit and said something that later he would fiercely regret.

When the people of Ammon prepared to go to war with Israel, the leaders of Gilead began looking for someone to lead them into battle. They recalled a certain "mighty man of valor" and went to Tob to get Jephthah.

AN OFFER FOR JEPHTHAH

The leaders of Gilead found Jephthah then ordered him to be their commander and lead them in a battle against the Ammonites. Having been hated by his brothers and expelled from his father's house, this did not go over very well with Jephthah. He questioned why they would come looking for his help just because they were in trouble.

The leaders of Gilead explained to Jephthah that their current trouble was the very reason they had come looking for him. In Judges 11:8 they explained that they wanted Jephthah to go with them and to fight for them!

What else did they say they wanted Jephthah to do? _____

_____

_____

_____

Had Jephthah heard them correctly? He must have wondered, because he asked them again: *"If you take me back home to fight against the people of Ammon, and the Lord delivers them to me, shall I be your head?"* The leaders reaffirmed their offer—if Jephthah fought for them he would be made head over the people of Gilead—and sealed it with *"the Lord as their witness."*

This phrase "the Lord will be a witness between us" carried a great deal of weight with the Israelites because it divinely substantiated a vow being made between two people or two parties. A vow being made before God would have to be honored...

Jephthah agreed to go with the leaders of Gilead and he was made the head and commander over them.

JEPTHAH'S NEGOTIATION

Jephthah's first action was to send messengers to the king of Ammon and ask them why they had come to fight against him in his land.

To negotiate for peace before a battle would have been in accordance with Mosaic Law. Jephthah must have been familiar with the principles governing warfare as outlined in Deuteronomy 20:10-20.

What reason did the king give for engaging the Israelites in battle? (Judges 11:13) _____

_____

_____

That message was sent back to Jephthah along with the king's request that the Israelites restore the land that they had taken from the Ammonites.

Jephthah again sent messengers to respond to the king of Ammon.

He explained that the land rightfully belonged to the Israelites because it was given to them by God. You might even detect a hint of sarcasm by Jephthah in v. 24 when he asks, *"Will you not possess whatever Chemosh your god gives you to possess? So whatever the Lord our God takes possession of before us, we will possess."*

Jephthah told the king of Ammon that he was wrong in fighting the Israelites and called on the Lord to judge between the two nations, but the king did not listen.

JEPHTHAH'S VOW

The Spirit of the Lord came upon Jephthah and he made his advance toward the Ammonites.

The Lord's Spirit coming over Jephthah set him apart as a judge and deliverer of the Israelites. That same divine action is described in Judges 3:10 with Othniel, Judges 6:34 with Gideon, and Judges 13:25 with Samson. The Spirit's augmentation of strength, courage, and zeal in those chosen leaders proved them to be qualified by the Lord.

Then Jephthah "opened his mouth" and made an unnecessary and foolish promise to the Lord:

"If You will indeed deliver the people of Ammon into my hands, then

it will be that whatever comes out of the doors of my house to meet me, when I return in peace from the people of Ammon, shall surely be the Lord's, and I will offer it up as a burnt offering."

In v. 32, what happened when Jephthah approached the Ammonites to engage in battle? _____

_____

_____

_____

There is much discussion over the translation of words found in v. 31. As one example, it has been debated that in the Hebrew text, the phrase found in v. 31 "...and I will offer it up as a burnt offering" can also be translated "...or I will offer it up as a burnt offering" suggesting that Jephthah intended to either give someone to the Lord or offer a burnt offering, depending on who or what came to meet him first.

JEPHTHAH'S RETURN HOME

Jephthah must have been elated over Israel's victory! After a long campaign with the Israelite army, certainly he was ready to return home to his family. Reading the story, as he approached Mizpah, you have to wonder if he was thinking about the vow he made to God and anxiously waiting to see what would come out of his house first, or if he had forgotten all about the foolish promise.

As he came walked toward his house, he saw someone coming down the path to meet him! It was a girl, dancing and playing a tambourine; a girl who Jephthah recognized as his precious daughter, his only child.

When Jephthah saw her, he tore his clothes and cried out in anguish, *"Alas, my daughter! You have brought me very low! You are among those who trouble me! For I have given my word to the Lord, and I cannot go back on it!"*

 Jephthah understood the gravity of his vow. As mentioned before, he must have been familiar with Mosaic Law. In Deuteronomy 23:21-23, Moses had explained to the Israelites the obligation of fulfilling a vow made to the Lord, and to not do so would be considered a sin.

HIS DAUGHTER'S RESPONSE

We aren't told the age of Jephthah's daughter, and we aren't given a description of her appearance, but we are given a glimpse of her **selfless** character when she responded to her father's heart-wrenching confession:

"My father, if you have given your word to the Lord, do to me according to what has gone out of your mouth, because the Lord has avenged you of your enemies, the people of Ammon."

There is no evidence of anger, refusal, or dispute. She simply acknowledged that a vow had been made, God had fulfilled His part, and her father needed to keep his word. She placed greater importance on her father's righteousness than on her own desires.

A HUMBLE REQUEST

Before repaying the vow, Jephthah's daughter asked that she be allowed to go into the mountains with her friends so that she could mourn her virginity. Jephthah agreed.

How much time did she request? (v. 37) _____

This appeal gives us one clue as to the nature of the sacrifice Jephthah intended to make concerning his daughter. He would not kill her, as human sacrifice is an abomination to the Lord (Leviticus 18:21; Deuteronomy 12:31; 18:10), rather he would dedicate his daughter for a lifetime of service to the Lord, essentially committing her to a permanent Nazarite vow, in the sense that she would be separate and holy to God for the remainder of her years.

His daughter mourned the fact that she would never marry, never know the love of a husband, and never have children. She mourned a life she would never experience and the dreams she would have to abandon.

While Jephthah's daughter sacrificed the life she might have hoped to live, Jephthah sacrificed the continuation of his name. With no other sons or daughters (Judges 11:34), his family line would come to an end: a matter of great significance to the Israelites.

A LIFE CELEBRATED

At the end of two months, Jephthah's daughter returned to her father and he carried out the vow he had made to God. She **submitted** to a fate that had been sealed by her father's impetuous offer.

In v. 39, there is another clue as to the nature of the sacrifice made by Jephthah's daughter, found in the words, *"She knew no man."* She remained a virgin, something that would not bear mentioning if her life had ended; rather the statement indicates that she lived a life of celibacy as a result of her father fulfilling his vow.

It became customary in Israel that for four days of each year the women would commemorate the daughter of Jephthah; which is yet another clue indicating the young woman was most likely not killed, in that the Israelites would not have annually paid tribute to an event that was an abomination to God. Rather, they celebrated the lifelong sacrifice of an honorable woman, who selflessly and submissively complied with the stipulations of an impulsive vow made by her father and Israel's judge, Jephthah.

In the Old Testament, who made a similar sacrifice when she gave her son to be reared by a priest for the remainder of his life? (1 Samuel 1:11) _____

Some people believe that Jephthah's daughter was literally sacrificed as a result of his vow. Although it is a possibility, one must consider whether Jephthah truly intended to take the life of another person and if God would have been pleased with such an action. In the end, regardless of the nature of the sacrifice, Jephthah's daughter teaches us that strength can be found through the virtues of selflessness and submission and for that she is memorialized forever in Scripture.

 STRENGTH TRAINING TIPS

1. **Sometimes life takes you down a road you didn't choose**

Throughout life there will be times that the road on which you're traveling abruptly ends. There may be a roadblock or construction up ahead, and you suddenly realize that you must change the route you've been following. In order to continue forward, you will need to choose a detour to get around whatever it is that has positioned itself in front of you.

Those detours may be the result of something wonderful: a job opportunity, a marriage, or a new baby.

But sometimes the detours are there because of something sad and deeply painful: an unfaithful spouse, a serious illness, or the death of someone dearly loved.

Detours can be difficult whatever the circumstance, and the key to finding happiness on a new course can be found in the heart of the traveler. It is the traveler who decides how she will adapt and the attitude she will possess in times of change. She can begin her journey down a new road with the question, "How can I use this detour to accomplish God's Will in my life?"

How does this apply to the story of Jepthah's daughter? __

_____

_____

_____

_____

_____

God knows each and every road we will travel. As His children, we demonstrate our faith by trusting in His providential care when we encounter detours throughout life.

What do we learn from Psalm 139:16 about the days of our lives and how do we find comfort in that? _____

_____

_____

When you are faced with a detour, what can you do to endure the change and become an even stronger traveler?

_____

_____

_____

2. **When we deny ourselves, we proclaim Christ**

To be a Christian is to practice self-denial. You can't be a follower of Christ and a follower of self: there can only be one leader! Can you imagine trying to get a group of children to play "Follow the Leader" with two leaders? It would be a disaster! There would be hurt feelings, fighting, yelling, and probably some tears.

When we deny ourselves, we refuse to follow our own wants and desires and completely surrender to the will of God. It means giving up everything for the cause of Christ, and Jesus tells us in Luke 9:23-24 that this is something that we do **daily**.

"Then He said to them all, 'If anyone desires to come after Me, let him deny himself, and take up his cross daily, and

follow Me. For whoever desires to save his life will lose it, but whoever loses his life for My sake will save it.'"

Others will see Christ reflected in your life when you make the decision every morning to fully submit to the Word of God and commit to obeying Him whatever the cost. It won't always be easy, but Jesus promises salvation to those who lose their lives for His sake!

What does it mean to "deny our selves?" _____

_____

_____

How does society today either challenge or encourage us in this effort? _____

_____

_____

In what ways can we practice self-denial daily? How does this make us stronger? _____

_____

_____

3.   **Submission does not equal weakness**

The idea of submission is misunderstood in today's world. It is often used in a negative sense, as a sign of weakness and implies a forced state of oppression. This is not the correct representation of the word as it is used in Scripture, by any means. Here is what you should know about submission:

- It is a choice. It is **never** forced upon someone!

- It requires strength.

- It is the quality of a good leader.

- It is mutual among Christians.

- It is love in action.

When you think of submission, think of Jesus Christ. Remember that He chose to die for the world in the ultimate demonstration of sacrificial love, and consider the strength that it took for Him to endure the cross. There was nothing weak about our Lord, and He is the perfect example of submission.

Submission isn't about "giving in"; it's about "lifting up"! It's about seeking the highest good for someone else and bringing them closer to God. Wives submit to husbands, husbands submit to wives, Christians submit to each other, and we all submit to the will of God.

In what way is submission characteristic of strength? _____

_____

_____

How does one provide leadership while also demonstrating submission? _____

_____

_____

4. **Live a life worthy of celebration**

Have you ever attended a funeral where, despite your sadness, you left feeling inspired? Where the words spoken gave testimony to a life well-lived for Christ? Where mourning and joy were partnered in honor of a faithful soul?

Although the sacrifice of Jephthah's daughter didn't involve her physical death, she did experience a loss of life in a sense. She lost the life she may have imagined for herself and gave up the hopes and dreams that could have made it a reality. Jephthah's daughter revealed great strength through her selfless and submissive actions and, as a result, her life was celebrated...and still is today!

Think about how you want to be remembered, not only in death, but also as your life interweaves with others from day to day. What would you like for people to say about the life you lived? _____

_____

_____

What do you want your legacy to be? _____

_____

_____

_____

We all should desire to live a life worthy of being celebrated!

Jesus' entire life was the picture of perfect service. I sometimes wonder what He would be doing if He were living in the world today. I believe with all of my heart He would be submitting to the Will of His Father and selflessly meeting the needs of everyone around Him. How do you think Jesus would spend His time if He were here today? Make a list of those things. Is there anything on the list that you might be able to incorporate in your daily schedule, even if on a smaller scale?

"The sacrifices of God are a broken spirit, a broken and contrite heart—these, O God, You will not despise." Psalm 51:17

◤TRAILMARKERS

1. Where do we find the account of Jephthah's daughter in the Bible? _____

   _____

2. What nation was oppressing Israel at this time in the land of Gilead? _____

   _____

3. Who was Jephthah? _____

   _____

   _____

4. Where did he and his family live? _____

   _____

5. What is the meaning of his name? _____

   _____

6. Why was Jephthah rejected by his siblings? _____

   _____

   _____

7. What did Jephthah do as a result? _____

   _____

   _____

8. Why did the elders of Gilead go to Tob to find Jephthah? __

_____

_____

9. What did they offer Jephthah and what was his response?

_____

_____

10. Before Jephthah went into battle against the Ammonites, what did he do first? _____

_____

11. What vow did Jephthah make to the Lord? _____

_____

_____

_____

_____

12. After Israel's victory over the Ammonites, who came out to meet Jephthah first upon his return home? _____

_____

_____

13. What was Jephthah's daughter's response to the vow he made? _____

_____

14. What request does she make to her father? _____

_____

_____

15. What was she mourning? _____

_____

_____

16. What does Judges 11:39 say Jephthah did upon the return of his daughter? _____

_____

_____

17. What custom was born as a result of Jephthah's daughter's sacrifice? _____

_____

18. How did Jephthah's daughter demonstrate selflessness? _

_____

_____

19. How did Jephthah's daughter demonstrate submissiveness? _____

_____

_____

_____

_____

20. What strength training lessons can we learn from Jephthah's daughter?

1.

2.

3.

4.

CHAPTER 7

HANNAH
PATIENT AND TRUSTWORTHY

LESSON TEXT /// 1 SAMUEL 1-2:10

Her desperate prayer is one of the greatest and most remembered in the Bible. She waited on the Lord to fulfill her most heartfelt desire, and when He blessed her with the gift she so desperately wanted, she honored the promise she had made to return that very same gift to the Lord.

I don't remember what brought me into her hospital room that night, but what I do recall is the look of fear on her face as I approached her bed. Her back, shoulders, and neck were rigid, keeping her from relaxing back against the pillow, and her hands grasped the top edge of the sheets that she had drawn up to her chin. She looked like a scared child but the whistle blowing silver and tattling lines revealed an age of near ninety. Trying to help calm her, I introduced myself and reassured her that we would be taking good care of her while in the hospital. Since she kept glancing toward the door, I asked if she had family that had come with her to the Emergency Room. At that, I heard a voice come from the far corner. It startled me because I hadn't seen anyone else in the room when I first entered.

"I'm here", someone said. I turned and saw an elderly man slowly rise from the couch in the darkness. Hearing his words, the patient sat up straighter and nervously responded, "Who is that?" Wondering the same thing, I asked the man his relation to the patient. "I'm her husband. We've been married 60 years.....she knows I'm here," and then (loud enough for the patient to hear) he said, "I'm always here." Then the remarkable: the patient eased back into her pillow, her hands loosened their hold on the sheet, and she closed her eyes as relief flooded her body. I say "flooded" because it spilled over to me as I simply stood next to her.

As this woman found comfort in the presence of her life partner, so we can find comfort in the ever presence of our Life Giver. He Himself has said, "I will never leave you nor forsake you" (Hebrews 13:5). Taking a deeper look at this Scripture, I found that the Greek word used here for "forsake" is egkataleipo. This word carries the meaning "to abandon, to desert, to leave helpless, to leave in straits, to leave in a lurch, or let one down." In the Greek text it is also preceded by three negatives which essentially multiplies the power of the promise, "I will not, I will not, I will not abandon you, desert you, leave you helpless, or let you down." Those are the words of our God, our Heavenly Father, and our Savior. He is always with us.

I forget this promise sometimes. Occasionally, my son jogs my memory as we drive down the road and he asks, "Mom, is God in the car with us right now?" On this particular night, it was a fearful patient and her loving husband who reminded me that I am never alone and the true peace that can be found in knowing that.

106

◥TRAILHEAD

Following Jephthah, the eighth judge of Israel, three more men served Israel as judges: Ibzan, Elon, and Abdon. After Abdon's death, the Israelites began to do evil again and the Lord allowed them to fall under Philistine oppression. At that same time we read in the Bible about the birth of a man named Samson; a man who would grow to become the twelfth judge of Israel.

How long did the period of oppression by the Philistines last? (Judges 13:1)

The time of the judges would soon be coming to an end, and Israel was approaching the threshold of a new era: the era of the kings. The Israelites continued to suffer at the hands of the Philistines and before long they would begin crying out for a king so they could be like the other nations around them (1 Samuel 8:4-5).

During that time Eli served Israel as the chief priest and lived in the tabernacle at Shiloh, with his two sons, who served as priests as well (corrupt and unfaithful priests, according to 1 Samuel 2:12). According to Mosaic Law, the Israelites were required to travel each year to the tabernacle for the purpose of worshipping God and offering sacrifices.

▰ THE TRUE STORY

HANNAH'S PLIGHT

Hannah lived with her husband, Elkanah, in the city of Ramathaim Zophim (or Ramah), which was located in the mountains of Ephraim. However, she didn't live there with her husband alone; Elkanah had a second wife by the name of Peninnah. Peninnah had been blessed with children, but Hannah had none of her own. The second verse of 1 Samuel 1 gives us this snapshot of Hannah and a first glimpse into the struggles of her personal life.

In Old Testament times, a barren woman was considered to be a failure in society. Some even believed she had been cursed by God, as she could not provide her husband with a child, particularly a son, which he needed to carry on his name. This cruel stigma must have made the emotional burden even more difficult to bear.

Elkanah made the yearly journey from his city to the tabernacle in Shiloh. When it came time for Elkanah to make his offering, he would give a portion of the resulting feast to Peninnah and all of her sons and daughters, but to Hannah he would give a double portion because he loved her in spite of the fact that she was unable to have children.

In 1 Samuel 1:5-6, what reason is given twice for why Hannah is barren? _____

_____

_____

There were three feasts the children of Israel were to honor annually in a place chosen by the Lord. According to Deuteronomy 16:16, those feasts were: the Feast of Unleavened Bread (also the observation of the Passover), the Feast of Weeks, and the Feast of Tabernacles. We are not told which feast was being observed by Elkanah.

It was not enough that Hannah was grieved because she was childless; Peninnah continually "provoked" her, causing Hannah to cry and not want to eat. We are not told specifically how Peninnah provoked Hannah—she may have insulted her, or made fun of her, or patronized her—but whatever she did, it made Hannah miserable.

"So it was, year by year..." (1 Samuel 1:7).

Hannah waited. Hannah endured. Hannah was **patient**. She never lashed out at Peninnah, and she never forsook the Lord.

Although he loved her, Elkanah did not fully understand her suffering. In 1 Samuel 1:8, he wants to know why she is crying, why she is not eating, and why her heart is so grieved. He even asks the question, *"Am I not better to you than ten sons?"* He certainly could not empathize with the deep longing Hannah had to be a mother.

HANNAH'S VOW

While in Shiloh, after they had finished eating and drinking, *"in bitterness of soul"* Hannah went to the tabernacle alone to pray. Eli, the priest, could see her from where he was seated by the doorpost of the tabernacle. Hannah was in anguish, sobbing, and began speaking to the Lord. She had reached the point of desperation in her desire for a child and in that moment she made a vow that would change her life.

"O Lord of hosts, if You will indeed look on the affliction of Your maidservant and remember me, and not forget Your maidservant, but will give Your maidservant a male child, then I will give him to the Lord all the days of his life, and no razor shall come upon his head" (1 Samuel 1:11).

Hannah promised that if God would give her a son, he would become a Nazarite and serve the Lord all the days of his life. If God gave her a son, she would give the boy back to God.

Eli watched Hannah as she prayed. Her mouth moved, but she was not making any sound, and from Eli's perspective the woman appeared to be drunk! He confronted Hannah and demanded, *"How long will you be drunk? Put your wine away from you!"*

Hannah explained that she had not been drinking any type of wine of intoxicating drink; rather she was pouring out her soul before the Lord! She told Eli that she was not a wicked woman, but that she had been speaking out of great trouble and sorrow.

Eli, recognizing that he sorely misjudged Hannah, told her to *"Go in peace"* and made the statement, *"The God of Israel grant your petition which you have asked of Him."* Eli may have been joining her in prayer, asking that God give her what she asked of Him or it may have been a prophecy that her prayer would be answered. Either way, Hannah *"went her way and ate, and her face was no longer sad."*

Hannah's heart had found contentment.

GOD REMEMBERS

Early the next morning, after worshipping the Lord, Elkanah and his family returned to their home in Ramah. *"Elkanah knew Hannah his wife...*

...and the Lord remembered her" (1 Samuel 1:19).

In time, Hannah conceived and gave birth to a son. She named him Samuel. In 1 Samuel 1:20, what reason does she give for choosing the name *Samuel*? _____

_____

_____

_____

 In Hebrew, the name Samuel literally means "gift of God."

HANNAH REMEMBERS

It came time for Elkanah to make his yearly trip to Shiloh, but this time Hannah did not go with him. She told her husband that she would not make the journey until Samuel was weaned. When that time came, she would take Samuel with her *"to appear before* the Lord" and then leave him at the tabernacle to *"remain there forever"* (1 Samuel 1:22).

She remembered her part of the vow.

Elkanah supported Hannah's decision, and she stayed home with little Samuel until he was weaned.

 Most commentaries agree that weaning would have occurred between the ages of three and five at this time in history.

After Hannah had weaned Samuel, she took him with her to the house of the Lord in Shiloh. She also brought three bulls ("a three-year-old bull" in some translations), one ephah of flour (or seven and a half gallons), and a skin of wine. They sacrificed the bull and brought Samuel to Eli the priest.

Hannah proved herself **trustworthy** by following through on the vow she had made to God and spoke these words to Eli:

"O my lord! As your soul lives, my lord, I am the woman who stood by you here, praying to the Lord. For this child I prayed, and the Lord has granted me my petition which I asked of Him. Therefore I also have lent him to the Lord; as long as he lives he shall be lent to the Lord." (1 Samuel 1:26-28)

After speaking these words, she worshipped the Lord.

HANNAH'S PRAYER

The second chapter of 1 Samuel begins with a prayer made by Hannah after turning over her son to be reared in the tabernacle with Eli.

What were the first words spoken by Hannah in v. 1? _____

_____

Read her entire prayer through 2:10. Her words are full of love, and you can feel her passion. They reflect the heart of a woman who honored God and who respected His power. This is not the prayer of a weak woman as we may have pictured Hannah to be in the first chapter. It is the prayer of a godly woman, a wise woman, and a strong woman.

_____

Hannah was blessed and the nation of Israel was blessed because of her patience and trustworthiness. She thought she was asking for a child for herself, but Israel received a judge and a prophet of unparalleled character and worth.

_____

STRENGTH TRAINING TIPS

1. **Understand that God is purposeful**

   Twice in the first chapter of 1 Samuel, in reference to Hannah, we read that *"the Lord had closed her womb."* God had a plan for Hannah, and there was a purpose behind the events in her life.

   It could be that God closed Hannah's womb in order to bring her to the point in which she would, through her tears, offer back to God the very thing she wanted most.

113

I wonder if Hannah would have willingly given young Samuel to God if the circumstances had been different. What if she had easily become pregnant and not ever had to reach the point of making a desperate vow?

As a result of God's hand in Hannah's life, Samuel was dedicated to the Lord's service his entire life. He became a great leader of God's people, as a judge, a prophet, and a priest. God had a purpose for Hannah even through her suffering.

My grandfather liked to refer to Romans 8:28 as "The Christian's Rocking Chair:"

"And we know that all things work together for good to those who love God, to those who are the called according to His purpose."

He used to say that Christians can just sit back and rock in the promise of those words.

How have you seen God's purpose demonstrated in your own life? _____

_____

Have you ever looked back on a difficult period in your life and been able to see how God was working to accomplish a greater plan? _____

_____

_____

2.   **Know that times of waiting can be followed by extraordinary blessings**

Waiting for things is not a curse. In fact, God will always use times of waiting to produce a blessing if you remain faithful in Him. Look at those times as opportunities to strengthen your faith and draw you closer to God. Then, be patient and trust in God's perfect timing.

After graduating from nursing school in Abilene, Texas, I remember praying every day that God would help me find a wonderful Christian man to marry. Little did I know, there was a certain man living in Nashville, Tennessee who was praying for God to help him find a Christian wife! While I was worried, thinking God was never going to answer my prayer, He was really working on how to get me from Texas to Tennessee and then to a worship service at Bellevue church of Christ that would forever change two lives!

"But those who wait on the Lord shall renew their strength; they shall mount up with wings like eagles, they shall run and not be weary, they shall walk and not faint" (Isaiah 40:31).

"The Lord is good to those who wait for Him, to the soul who seeks Him" (Lamentations 3:25).

Why might we have to wait for certain things in our lives? _

_____

_____

_____

How can you become stronger during times of waiting? ___

_____

_____

_____

God **will** make it worth the wait.

Make a list of the greatest blessings in your life. How many of those blessings came after a time of waiting? Looking back, can you see evidence of God's perfect timing? If you included the names of any people on your list, if it is possible, take the time today to let them know that they are one of your greatest blessings!

3. **Lean on God in times of sorrow and desperation**

The question, "Why does God allow suffering?" has been asked, discussed, studied and debated for thousands of years. When considering the answer, it is important to keep in mind these truths: God is sovereign, He is purposeful, He loves us, and He is always good. When we are hurting, He is hurting with us. When our hearts are breaking, His heart is breaking, too. In our times of sorrow and desperation, God is *always* there. He will not, He will not, He will not ever leave us.

Sometimes suffering is a result of the natural course of life on Earth. With the fall of man in the Garden, sin, sickness, death, and pain entered the world; and these will plague man until Jesus comes again. Suffering may also be brought about by the devil, whose intent is evil and motive is selfish. Finally, God may allow suffering in order to accomplish His divine purpose in our lives. In Psalm

119:67-71, David wrote that as a result of his affliction, he was made faithful and learned the statutes of God.

Regardless of the source, in times of suffering we can reflect on the wise words of Solomon in Proverbs 3:5, *"Trust in the Lord with all your heart, and lean not on your own understanding."*

Never lose faith in God and always believe in His ability to use our times of sorrow and desperation according to His perfect will. Remember that *"His ways are higher than our ways"* (Isaiah 55:8-9).

When faced with struggles, what can we learn from the phrases *"lean not on your own understanding"* and *"His ways are higher than our ways"*? _____

_____

_____

In the book of James, we are told to be joyful when we encounter trials. Why can we find joy in those times, according to James 1:2-4? _____

_____

_____

4.   **Be a woman who keeps her promises**

Following through on promises is important for building trust in every relationship. This applies to **all** promises, from the life-long promise you make to be faithful to your spouse, to the seemingly small promise that you will return a phone call. When you say you are going to do something....do it!

If you continually have an excuse for not being able to keep a promise, your trustworthiness begins to crumble and others will see that they simply cannot depend on you. This is especially dangerous for the Christian. If others cannot trust you in matters of this life, how can they trust you in matters of your faith?

Be a woman who keeps her promises, not only to show that you are worthy of trust, but also because you represent the Truth of the Gospel.

How does keeping our promises establish trust? _____

_____

_____

Why is it important to be considered trustworthy? _____

_____

_____

What does the Bible teach us about God keeping His promises? (Read Numbers 23:19, Joshua 21:45, Titus 1:2, and Hebrews 10:23) _____

_____

_____

"For the eyes of the Lord run to and fro throughout the whole earth to show Himself strong on behalf of those whose heart is loyal to Him." 2 Chronicles 16:9a

◤TRAILMARKERS

1. Where can you read the account of Hannah in the Bible? __
   _____

2. Why were the Israelites crying out for a king? _____
   _____
   _____

3. Who was Eli? _____
   _____

4. What was the name of Hannah's husband? _____

5. What was Hannah's struggle? _____
   _____

6. What was the name of the other wife who treated Hannah
   so cruelly? _____

7. How did Hannah physically react to her situation? _____
   _____

8. How did Elkanah respond to Hannah's suffering? _____
   _____
   _____
   _____

9. What did Hannah's "bitterness of soul" lead her to do? ___
   _____
   _____

10. What did she vow? _____
    _____
    _____

11. What did Eli think about Hannah as he watched her pray?

_____

_____

12. After Hannah explained her plight to Eli, what did he tell her? _____

_____

13. How is Hannah described after her prayer? _____

_____

_____

14. How did God answer Hannah's prayer? _____

_____

_____

15. What does the name Samuel mean? _____

_____

16. How long did Hannah keep Samuel before she took him with her on the journey to the tabernacle in Shiloh?) _____

_____

17. How did Hannah keep her promise to God? _____

_____

_____

_____

_____

18. How did Hannah demonstrate patience? _____

_____

_____

_____

_____

19. What does she teach us about being trustworthy? _____

   _____

   _____

   _____

20. List four strength training tips we learn from the account of Hannah:

   1.

   2.

   3.

   4.

CHAPTER 8

ABIGAIL
DISCERNING AND HUMBLE

LESSON TEXT /// 1 SAMUEL 25

When her foolish husband insulted the future king of Israel and put the safety of their household at stake, Abigail immediately took matters into her own hands. Her good judgment and humble spirit not only saved her family, but changed her life forever.

There are some things you just can't rush. It may be a race with the clock to get the kids off to school in the morning, but when it's time to let the dog out you may as well forget the time. Murray, our Golden Retriever, used to take as long as he needed outside, regardless of his family's schedule constraints. One day, I stood in the driveway holding my cup of coffee, leaving the whirlwind that is our morning routine for a few minutes, while Murray scrutinized the lawn.

It began to rain. Not a downpour, but an occasional drop. Then as I was about to take a sip of my coffee, one raindrop plopped right into the middle of my cup. It struck me as funny there in that moment. I found myself smiling at the thought of my regular coffee being transformed into a "beverage of perfection" having been infused with a little gift from Heaven.

The thought stayed with me all morning, and I couldn't get out of my head the idea that...I am the coffee! Standing there in the driveway, in my suburban neighborhood, wearing jeans, polka-dot flip flops, a sweatshirt, glasses, and my hair in a messy bun, with three children inside probably sword fighting with toaster strudels; I realized that I am about as Medium Roast as you get. But I have a drop of something perfect that takes me to another level. I have Jesus, God's perfect Son, who lives in my heart! While I am flawed in many ways, His presence there permeates through every aspect of my life and transforms me from something regular into something special....a true Special Roast!

So from now on when you order your grande white chocolate latte, non-fat, no whip (or whatever your persuasion)...think about your own personal blend and what can happen when you add a single drop of perfection.

◥TRAILHEAD

Saul was reigning on the throne over Israel, but because of his disobedience, the Lord had rejected him as king (1 Samuel 15:24-26). Samuel followed the words of the Lord and anointed a shepherd boy named David to serve in the future as God's chosen king.

When Saul felt troubled, it was young David came and played music to calm his spirit; and it was David who defeated the giant Goliath and caused the Philistine army to run away from the

Israelites, but David would not remain in good favor with King Saul.

As David grew in popularity with the people, Saul became consumed with jealously. He knew the Lord was with David and that made him very afraid. Saul began to look for ways to end David's life.

 In 1 Samuel 18-19, Saul attempted twelve different times to take David's life!

David ran away from Saul and hid in various places throughout the wilderness. During that time, David was joined by 400 men and became captain over them.

In 1 Samuel 22:2, describe the characteristics of those men. _____

The number of men who banned together with David in the wilderness rose to six hundred (1 Samuel 23:13), and together they fought the enemies of the Israelites while continuing to foil Saul's murderous plots against the future king.

 The psalms written by David are reflective of the events and emotions he was experiencing at particular times in his life. Several of them were written during the time that Saul was threatening his life. Read Psalm 59, and imagine David fearful for his life and praying for God's protection.

✒ THE TRUE STORY

A RICH MAN

David and his men were in the wilderness when they heard that a man named Nabal was in the city of Carmel shearing his sheep. Nabal lived in Maon, north of Carmel where he conducted his business, and was known throughout the area as a very wealthy man. He had three thousand sheep and one thousand goats!

Nabal was married to woman named Abigail, described in 1 Samuel 25:3 as *"a woman of good understanding and beautiful appearance."* Nabal, on the other hand, is characterized as being *"harsh and evil in his doings."*

In Hebrew, the name Abigail means "father's joy" and Nabal means "fool" or "senseless." It is evident when reading this account in 1 Samuel 25 that Nabal truly lives up to his name!

DAVID'S REQUEST

David and his men needed food and other provisions, so he sent for ten young men and gave them a message to take to Nabal in the city of Carmel. First, David instructed the men to greet Nabal on his behalf and then to offer peace to Nabal, his house, and all his possessions.

Then David told the ten messengers to explain to Nabal how his shepherds had been kept from harm in the wilderness and that nothing was missing from them throughout the time they were in Carmel. David even encouraged Nabal to ask the shepherds himself in order to confirm the story.

David asked that Nabal be gracious to him and his men because it was a feast day and because they had provided protection for Nabal's shepherds and herds. His request to Nabal was, *"Please give whatever comes to your hand to your servants and to your son David."*

We are not specifically told what event is being honored with the feast mentioned in v. 8, but it is possible the people were celebrating the time of sheep shearing which was considered a "harvest" of sorts to the sheep rancher.

THE FOOLISH RESPONSE

David's men delivered the message to Nabal and waited for his response. When Nabal answered them he said, *"Who is David, and who is the son of Jesse? There are many servants nowadays who break away each one from his master. Shall I then take my bread and my water and my meat that I have killed for my shearers, and give it to men when I do not know where they are from?"*

First, Nabal insulted David by refusing to recognize him when David was a prominent figure and known all throughout Israel (1 Samuel 18:5-7). Then, Nabal compared David to *"just another servant running away from his master"* when David was only running from Saul in an effort to save his own life. Finally, Nabal completely rejected David's request for help when in fact he was benefitting from a harvest that David and his men helped to secure. Nabal really showed his true colors!

---

1 Samuel 25:11 is a great reflection of Nabal's selfish character. Count how many times he uses the words "I" and "my" in his response to David. _____

DAVID'S REACTION

David's messengers returned and told him all the words spoken by Nabal. David was deeply insulted and extremely angry! He said to his men, *"Surely in vain I have protected all that this fellow has in the wilderness, so that nothing was missed of all that belongs to him. And he has repaid me evil for good. May God do so, and more also, to the enemies of David, if I leave one male of all who belong to him by morning light."*

David armed himself with his sword and ordered 400 of his men to do likewise, leaving 200 men to guard their supplies. David was ready to fight!

In the previous chapter, 1 Samuel 24, David spared Saul's life and extended respect and kindness to the very man who sought to kill him! However, when offended by a rude and wealthy man, he immediately prepared to attack him and his family. David was not acting wisely or according to the character of a godly man.

ABIGAIL INFORMED

One of Nabal's young shepherds had heard how his master had responded to David's messengers, and he explained the entire story to Nabal's wife, Abigail. He told her what David had requested and how Nabal had criticized him and refused to offer any help. The shepherd described how David and his men had protected the shepherds in the wilderness by acting as *"a wall around them by day and night while they kept their sheep."*

The young man told Abigail that Nabal was such a scoundrel that no one could speak to him, and he encouraged her to carefully consider what should be done because Nabal and his entire household were in danger.

ABIGAIL'S ACTION

Abigail found herself in a position that required her to make an important judgment: Should she stand behind her husband and his foolish decision or take the necessary action to save her family and regain favor with David? A **discerning** woman, Abigail made her decision and began to act quickly. She took two hundred loaves of bread, two wineskins, five sheep already dressed, five quarts of roasted grain, one hundred clusters of raisins, and two hundred cakes of figs, and loaded them on donkeys.

She sent servants ahead of her to meet David and told nothing to her husband Nabal.

Abigail rode under cover of a hill on her donkey and encountered

David and his army of men as they descended the hillside toward her. When she saw David, she swiftly dismounted from the donkey, fell on her face before him, and **humbly** bowed to the ground.

ABIGAIL'S SPEECH

"On me, my lord, on me let this iniquity be! And please let your maidservant speak in your ears, and hear the words of your maidservant."

With those words, Abigail began her appeal to David for the sake of her husband and her household (1 Samuel 25:24-31). She accepted complete responsibility for the situation, and while she pointed out her husband's foolishness, she did not rest the blame on his shoulders.

Next, she pointed out that, through her intercession, the Lord was holding him back from causing bloodshed and avenging himself with his own hand. Then she presented the gifts that she brought for the men and reminded David that the Lord would give him an enduring house in Israel if he remained faithful. Abigail assured David that the Lord would protect him from Saul and *"sling out, as from the pocket of a sling,"* the lives of his enemies.

Notice that Abigail described how the Lord would remove David's enemies using a reference to a sling, a significant reminder from David's past. She knew how David had defeated the giant Goliath, although the odds had not been in his favor. God saved him then...and God would save him now.

Finally, Abigail told David that God would keep His promise and make him the appointed ruler over Israel, but he would experience grief and a troubled heart if he shed blood without cause, having avenged himself. She concluded her plea with the request that David remember her in the future when the Lord rewarded him.

DAVID'S REACTION

David listened and he praised God for Abigail's intervention! He blessed her and the advice she gave! David realized that he had been prevented from committing a drastic sin because of the Abigail.

What did David tell her would have happened by morning light had she not hurried to meet him (vv. 32-34)? _____

_____

_____

David took from Abigail all she had brought and then said to her, *"Go in peace to your house. See I have heeded your voice and respected your person."*

Abigail had saved her husband, saved her home, and saved the lives of many men in her household.

NABAL'S FATE

While Abigail had been away, desperately trying to fix the dangerous situation Nabal had created, Nabal had been at home holding a feast, "like the feast of a king." Abigail returned and found her husband drunk, and in her discernment thought it best not to tell him anything until the morning.

When morning came and "the wine had gone from Nabal," Abigail told him everything. According to v. 37, "Nabal's heart died within him and he became like a stone," and ten days later the Lord struck Nabal and he died.

It may be that upon hearing all that Abigail said, Nabal experienced a heart attack or a stroke that left him in a comatose state.

THE HAPPY ENDING

When David heard about the death of Nabal, he praised God again for having kept him from evil and for repaying Nabal the wickedness he had demonstrated.

David sent for Abigail and proposed to her! When his servants told her that they had come to Carmel to ask that she become David's wife, Abigail humbly bowed her face to the ground and said, *"Here is your maidservant, a servant to wash the feet of the servants of my lord."*

In Bible times, the washing of someone's feet was an outward display of servitude. In John 13:1-20, who performed this act in an extraordinary example of humility and sacrificial love? _____

Then beautiful Abigail became the wife of a future king.

 STRENGTH TRAINING TIPS

1. **Use good judgment in everyday moments**

When Abigail heard how Nabal had responded to David's request, she didn't hesitate to act, and made a good judgment in a difficult situation!

How we live moment to moment prepares us for problems and challenges we will encounter in our lives. When we find ourselves in a difficult situation, how we respond to that situation has been conditioned by how we have handled other "everyday" moments in our lives.

Faced with a crisis or a difficult decision, the best time to begin formulating a response is not in the heat of the moment...you might not have time to carefully consider the options, or to consult the Scriptures for the answer. But if you are continually filling your heart and mind with the Word of God and are seeking God's guidance through prayer, moment to moment, when those tough situations present themselves, you are better prepared to make good judgments.

What moments do you come across in day-to-day life that require using good judgment? _____

_____

_____

How can using discernment in every day moments help when it comes to facing a crisis? _____

_____

_____

When faced with decision-making moments, keep this acronym in mind:

M*indful*

O*f*

M*y*

E*ternity*

N*ot*

T*emporary*

S*atisfaction*

2.   **Be responsible for your own faith**

"For we must all appear before the judgment seat of Christ, that each one may receive the things done in the body, according to what he has done, whether good or bad" (2 Corinthians 5:10).

I come from a faithful Christian family, I attend worship services with a faithful congregation, I am blessed to be married to a faithful husband. But no measure of the faith that surrounds me will save me when I stand before God, if I am not faithful.

The verse written above tells us that we all must appear before the judgment seat of Christ and give an account for what we did in this life. We read in Ezekiel 18:20, that each person will bear his own sin: *"the righteousness of the righteous shall be upon himself, and the wickedness of the wicked shall be upon himself."*

Keeping that in mind, be motivated by the words of Paul to the church at Philippi, *"Therefore, my beloved, as you have always obeyed, not as in my presence only, but now much more in my absence, **work out your own salvation with fear and trembling**"* (Philippians 2:12).

The phrase "work out" does not mean "figure out." There is no guessing as to how we obtain salvation; the Bible very clearly tells us! But to *"work out"* in the context it is used here means to achieve, accomplish, or complete something thoroughly, from the Greek word *katergazomai*. We are to continue obeying and to keep trying to live a Christ-like life, as we submit to the process of sanctification by the Holy Spirit, through the Word of God. This is the responsibility of each individual Christian and should be done in awe and reverence of God's power.

Describe how Abigail's actions teach us that we should be responsible for our own faith. _____

_____

_____

In what ways are you demonstrating responsibility for your own faith? _____

_____

_____

3.   **Be a godly example to the man in your life**

Abigail is described as *"beautiful"* and *"a woman of good understanding"* – a stark contrast to the foolish man to whom she was married. We know from reading the text that Nabal was *"harsh and evil,"* he insulted a reputable man who had shown him kindness, and he was a drunk; but despite her husband, Abigail was a woman of faith!

There is no evidence from the Scripture that Abigail was physically abused by her husband, and I would advise any woman in that situation to seek help immediately. In Abigail's case, she endured a marriage to a man who was selfish, rude, and unfaithful to God. Nevertheless, Abigail lived righteously, possibly with a hope for what Peter wrote about many years later in 1 Peter 3:1-2, *"Wives, likewise, be submissive to your own husbands, that even if some do not obey the word, they, without a word, may be won by the conduct of their wives, when they observe your chaste conduct accompanied by fear,"* or asking herself the same question Paul posed in 1 Corinthians 7:16, *"For how do you know, O wife, whether you will save your husband?"*

Abigail was a godly example, not only to Nabal, but to her entire household. She lived the words of Christ in Matthew 5:16, *"Let your light so shine before men, that they may see your good works and glorify your Father in Heaven."*

Don't underestimate the effect your shining light can have on others!

How do we know from the text that Abigail had a positive impact on all those living in her home? _____

_____

_____

In what ways can a wife be a godly example to her husband? _____

_____

_____

4. **Don't be too beautiful to bow**

Abigail humbly fell at the feet of David. Consider this definition of the word humble: *"having or showing a modest or low view of one's own importance; modest in behavior, attitude, or spirit; not arrogant or proud."*

The Bible teaches us a great deal on the subject of humility. Think about these verses:

"By humility and the fear of the Lord are riches and honor and life" (Proverbs 22:4).

"For I say, through the grace given to me, to everyone who is among you, not to think of himself more highly than he ought to think, but to think soberly, as God has dealt to each one a measure of faith" (Romans 12:3).

"Let nothing be done through selfish ambition or conceit, but in lowliness of mind let each esteem others better than himself. Let each of you look out not only for his own interests, but also for the interests of others" (Philippians 2:3-4).

"Humble yourselves in the sight of the Lord, and He will lift you up" (James 4:10).

Abigail put the interests of her household above her own; she willingly bore the blame for Nabal's actions; she pleaded for David's forgiveness; and she respectfully pointed out the plans that God had for David's future. She may have been beautiful, and she may have been wealthy, but it was because of her humility that she was later *"lifted up"* and became the wife of God's chosen king. Like Abigail, we humbly bow at the feet of our King, knowing that it is only the soul-cleansing blood of His perfect Son that can lift us up from the ugliness sin and make us beautiful.

In what situations might you be able to demonstrate humility in your life? _____

_____

_____

How does becoming more humble make you stronger? ___

_____

_____

The psalms of David are beautiful expressions of love, praise, thanksgiving, sadness, wisdom, and humility. I encourage you, in your time of personal Bible study, to practice creating your own. Talking to God through a written psalm is thought provoking, emotional, and humbling. This is a challenging activity... but you will be uplifted by it!

"Do not be overcome by evil, but overcome evil with good."
Romans 12:21

◤TRAILMARKERS

1. Where can you read the account of Abigail in the Bible? ___

_____

2.   What was the history of David and Saul leading up to this
     point? _____

     _____

     _____

     _____

     _____

3.   What does the name Abigail mean in Hebrew? _____

     _____

4.   Who was Abigail's husband? _____

     _____

5.   What does his name mean? _____

     _____

6.   What did David ask of Nabal? _____

     _____

7.   Why did David think Nabal should give him what he asked?

     _____

     _____

8.   What was Nabal's response? _____

     _____

     _____

9.   What did David plan to do to Nabal and his household? ___

     _____

     _____

10. How does Abigail find out about the situation? _____

     _____

     _____

11.　What does Abigail do? _____

_____

_____

_____

12.　What was David's response to Abigail? _____

_____

_____

13.　When Abigail returned home, in what state did she find her husband? _____

_____

_____

14.　Did Abigail tell her husband what she did? _____

_____

15.　What happened to Nabal? _____

_____

16.　After David heard of Nabal's death, what did he do? _____

_____

_____

_____

17.　What was the meaning of Abigail's response in v. 41? ___

_____

_____

_____

18.　How did Abigail use discernment in her situation? _____

_____

_____

_____

19.   How did Abigail demonstrate humility? _____

      _____

      _____

      _____

20.   What strength training tips can we learn from Abigail?

      1.

      2.

      3.

      4.

CHAPTER 9

THE WOMAN OF ABEL

WISE AND PEACEMAKING

LESSON TEXT /// 2 SAMUEL 20:1-22

The timely wisdom and fearless peace-making efforts of this "nameless wonder" thwarted the advances of a brutal army commander on a deadly mission. Known only as "The Woman of Abel," her actions ultimately prevented a war and saved her city from destruction.

With my head turned toward the sky, eyes closed, hands sinking in the sand behind me, I drank in the salty ocean air. Deep gulps...like a thirsty child at a playground water fountain. It felt so good.

I sat there for a moment, enveloped by the beauty of the scene, and gradually I could feel myself begin to let go of the world: the worry and fear that I seem to harbor being pushed out of my mind by an overwhelming awareness of my Creator.

Deep in the process of emptying myself, I opened my eyes just in time to see my three children running toward the ocean. They bounded through the ankle-deep, shin-deep, then knee-deep waves, and dove right into the water. I saw them float, swim, and race each other back to shore. I watched them play in the sand: digging, building, writing, and burying themselves. Then back to the water.

I realized that while I was emptying...they were filling.

There, in the presence of God's undeniable power and glory, I was giving up my weaknesses, handing over my struggles, and letting God's peace take control. Emptying.

My children, on the other hand, were jumping in and swimming around. Filling.

It made me think about how those two actions manifest themselves in my life as a Christian.

*Being **emptied** of the world and being **filled** with the Spirit.*

Both needed...both necessary.

I should live a life of sacrifice and not be conformed to this world. I should turn my burdens over to God. The emptying.

But also, I should be submerged in God's love and grace. I should saturate myself in His Word. The filling.

Quietly sitting in the sand and thinking about how much God has given me, reflecting on His magnificence is important, it helps me refocus and recharge; but, at some point, it's equally important to put aside inhibition, run full force into the water, and outright plunge into His greatness. James wrote about this through inspiration telling his readers they should be *"doers of the word and not hearers only"* in James 1:22.

I don't want to be just a sand sitter...I want to be a wave rider!

And with that, I grabbed my boogie board and raced my kids to the water.

◤TRAILHEAD

The death of Saul brought much dissension between the northern tribes of Israel and southern tribe of Judah. The house of Saul gained support from the northern tribes while Judah showed loyalty to the house of David; and there was a long war between the two houses. In 2 Samuel 3:1, we read, "David grew _____ and _____, and the house of Saul grew _____ and _____."

After the murder of Saul's son Ishbosheth, the elders of Israel approached David and anointed him king over all of Israel.

David had a son Absalom who became greedy for the throne and committed an act of treason against his own father. He "stole the hearts" of the men of Israel by unlawfully acting as their judge, and over time he assembled a rebellion. Absalom was killed by Joab, the commander of David's army, and his supporters fled.

Joab was the nephew of David, the commander of David's army, a skillful warrior, and brutal in his dealings with opposition. He murdered Abner, who had left the position as commander of Saul's army and pledged his allegiance to David; he carried out David's evil plot against Uriah; and he killed David's son

143

Absalom when David had ordered that Absalom's life be spared. David replaced Joab, as commander of his army, with another of his nephews named Amasa, who had served as captain of Absalom's army in the revolt against David. It may have been that David chose Amasa in an effort to unite the northern and southern tribes or that he had completely lost trust in Joab.

Following Absalom's death, David was again restored as king over all of Israel only to have his throne challenged again by man named Sheba. Every man of Israel deserted King David and followed the rebel Sheba, who came from Saul's tribe of Benjamin.

▰ THE TRUE STORY

SHEBA'S REVOLT

"We have no share in David, nor do we have inheritance in the son of Jesse; every man to his tents, O Israel!"

Sheba blew a trumpet and then spoke those words in a battle cry to rally the men of Israel against King David. Every man of Israel followed Sheba, but the men of Judah remained loyal to their king.

---

2 Samuel 20:3 makes an interesting reference to ten concubines of David. The Scripture says that David took the concubines "whom he had left to keep the house, and put them in seclusion and supported them, but did not go in to them. So they were shut up to the day of their death, living in widowhood." Read 2 Samuel 15:13-16 and then 2 Samuel 16:21-22 to find out who those women were and how they came to suffer such a fate.

DAVID'S ORDERS

David commanded Amasa to assemble the men of Judah over the course of three days and then return to him. Amasa left to complete the task but delayed longer than the time allotted, and David became worried.

He called for Abishai, a proven military leader and brother of Joab, and voiced his concern: *"Now Sheba the son of Bichri will do us more harm than Absalom. Take your lord's servants and pursue him, lest he find for himself fortified cities, and escape us."*

Joab somehow received word of David's order and gathered his men, the Cherethites, the Pelethites, and all the mighty men, and went out of Jerusalem to pursue Sheba, along with Joab's brother, Abishai.

The Cherethites, the Pelethites, and the mighty men made up an army that had pledged devotion to David during the time he had spent in the wilderness running from Saul. The "mighty men" referred to the 600 men who had followed David from Gath, the hometown of Goliath, and were also known as the Gittites. Many scholars believe these men, along with the Cherethites and Pelethites, were Philistine warriors who chose to serve King David with extraordinary loyalty (2 Samuel 8:18; 15:18; 20:7, 1 Kings 1:38).

AMASA'S FATE

When Joab, Abishai, and their army reached the large stone in Gibeon, they found Amasa there. Joab, dressed in full battle armor, stepped toward Amasa and as he did his sword fell out of its sheath. Joab asked, *"Are you in health, my brother?"* and as a customary greeting and display of friendship, he took Amasa by the beard with his right hand to kiss him.

However, Amasa did not notice the fallen sword that Joab picked up with his other hand and Joab struck the unsuspecting Amasa in the stomach and killed him. Then Joab and Abishai, demonstrating no remorse for the murder of their cousin, left to continue chasing Sheba.

One of Joab's men who stood near Amasa called out, *"Whoever favors Joab and whoever is for David—follow Joab!"* But the others stood frozen in horror as Amasa still lay dying in the middle of the road. So the men moved the body of Amasa from the highway to a field and threw a piece of clothing over him. At that point, all of the men rejoined Joab and the pursuit of Sheba.

SHEBA FOUND

Sheba had made his way through the tribes of Israel, as well as through the region of the Berites where he found additional recruits to join his cause, and he finally reached the northern city of Abel-Beth-maachah, in the region of Dan. Sheba took cover there and hid within the fortified walls of the city.

Joab and his army reached Abel-Beth-maachah and began to lay siege on the city. They built a siege mound against the city and began battering the walls in order to tear them down!

*A **siege tower** was constructed by an attacking army in order to gain access to the upper portion of the wall outside of a besieged city. A **siege mound** served the same purpose but was made up of earth, stones, or trees.*

A BATTLE STOPPED

All of a sudden, from amid the yelling voices of men and sounds of impending battle, a woman was heard crying out from the city, *"Hear, hear! Please say to Joab, 'Come nearby that I may speak with you.'"*

Joab came to speak with the woman and she asked, *"Are you Joab?"* He responded, *"I am."* She said to him, *"Hear the words of your maidservant,"* and Joab replied, *"I am listening."*

The wise woman explained to Joab how, in the past, the city of Abel had been regarded as a place for seeking guidance in settling disputes. She told him that in the city of Abel-Beth-maachah she was among the peaceable and faithful in Israel and pointed out to him that he was about to destroy one of Israel's chief cities. In an effort to make peace and save her city, she posed the question to Joab, *"Why would you swallow up the inheritance of the Lord?"*

The wise woman must have been familiar with the Law and understood that Joab should not attack a city without first proclaiming an offer of peace (Deuteronomy 20:10-11).

147

Joab, not known for defending his actions in the past, began to defend himself in the presence of the woman and answered, *"Far be it, far be it from me, that I should swallow up or destroy! That is not so."* He told the woman about Sheba and how he was leading a revolt against King David. *"Deliver him only,"* Joab requested, *"and I will depart from the city."*

So the woman said to Joab, *"Watch, his head will be thrown to you over the wall."*

The woman, in her wisdom, returned to the people of her city and relayed the offer of Joab. The head of Sheba, son of Bichri, was cut off and thrown over the wall. Joab blew a trumpet, and all the army withdrew from the city.

Joab's mission was accomplished, the city of Abel-Beth-maachah remained standing, and many innocent lives were saved because of one woman.

STRENGTH TRAINING TIPS

1. **Ask for wisdom**

    Wisdom comes from God (Proverbs 2:6), and if we ask Him for it, He will give it to us! (James 1:5)

    In 1 Kings 3:5-15, read what happened to King Solomon when he asked God for an *"understanding heart"* and the ability to discern between good and evil. God answered his prayer and richly blessed him because of his request. Later, in the book of Proverbs, Solomon wrote much about the value of wisdom.

In Proverbs 2:1-20, Solomon lists two of wisdom's greatest benefits. What are they? (vv. 5-6 and vv. 11-12a) _____

_____

Knowing those benefits, how can wisdom help you grow in strength? _____

_____

_____

2. **Increase your knowledge...and apply it! (It's not enough just to have it)**

Knowledge is "knowing the facts," but wisdom is being able to apply what you know in real life situations. Solomon wrote that a wise person uses their knowledge in the right way (Proverbs 15:2).

The woman of Abel was knowledgeable of the Law, but it was when she took what she knew and used it to deter Joab's attack that she demonstrated wisdom. You may be brimming with Bible facts, which is wonderful. But to be wise like the woman of Abel, when the time and intent is right, you have to climb up on the wall and shout out what you know!

Paul explained to Timothy in 2 Timothy 3:14-15 that he should continue in his learning and in the knowledge of the Holy Scriptures, *"which are able to make you wise for salvation through faith which is in Christ Jesus."* Notice that Paul said the Scriptures are *"**able** to make you wise."* Study and know them, but wisdom will come when you apply them to your life through faith.

How do you increase your Bible knowledge? _____

_____

How are you applying that knowledge in your daily life?
How are you sharing it with others? _____

_____

_____

3.   **Seek peace**

The woman of Abel had a clear motive: She wanted a
peaceful resolution in order to save her city from destruction.

The Bible tells us that we should be peace-seeking people:

"Depart from evil and do good; seek peace and pursue it"
(Psalm 34:14).

*"Blessed are the peacemakers, for they shall be called sons
of God"* (Matthew 5:9).

*"If it is possible, as much as depends on you, live peaceably
with all men"* (Romans 12:18).

*"Pursue peace with all people, and holiness; without which
no one will see the Lord"* (Hebrews 12:14).

Why is it important for Christians to be peacemakers? ____

_____

_____

_____

_____

_____

How is strength found through peace? _____

_____

_____

_____

*Spread peace by heading up a "Random Act of Kindness"
project in your home. Give each family member five pieces
of white paper that are about the size of a dollar bill. These will be
the R.A.O.K. tickets. Let everyone sign and decorate their own
tickets. Then, over the next couple of weeks, each person looks for
opportunities to perform five acts of kindness for other family
members. When they do, they leave a ticket at the scene. After
trying this at home, make new tickets, add a Scripture and an
invitation to worship, and take this project out into the community!*

4.   **Have a spirit of fearlessness**

*"The Lord is my light and my salvation; whom shall I fear?
The Lord is the strength of my life; of whom shall I be
afraid?"* (Psalm 27:1).

*"So we may boldly say: 'The Lord is my helper; I will not fear,
what can man do to me?'"* (Hebrews 13:6).

There are moments in life that require fearlessness:
standing up for something that is right, speaking out
against an injustice, taking advantage of an opportunity;
and when those moments come, remember that God is on

your side. You don't have to be afraid! Sometimes you just have to put aside inhibition, run full force toward the water, and then plunge into the "doing!"

Have you ever been in a situation that required you to be fearless? Have you seen someone, in a big way or small way, demonstrate a spirit of fearlessness? _____

_____

How can you create a spirit of fearlessness within yourself?

_____

_____

Sometimes a measure of fearlessness can result in great things. In the life of the woman of Abel, it saved an entire city!

 "You know, sometimes all you need is twenty seconds of insane courage. Just literally seconds of just embarrassing bravery. And I promise you, something great will come of it." (Benjamin Mee in the movie We Bought a Zoo)

"Listen to counsel and receive instruction, that you may be wise in your latter days." Proverbs 19:20

⊓TRAILMARKERS

1. Where can you find the account of the woman of Abel in the Bible? _____

2. What is the relationship between the northern and southern regions of Israel at this time? _____

_____

3. Who is king over Israel at this time? _____

_____

4. Who started a revolt and drew the men of Israel away from following after King David? _____

5. David calls on the head of his army, _____, to pursue the rebels; and he gives him _____ days to complete the task.

6. Who is sent next when the mission is not accomplished within the appointed time? _____

_____

7. Who decides to go along too, and whom does he bring with him? _____

_____

8. Where do David's men find Amasa? _____

_____

9. What terrible action is taken by Joab when he faces Amasa? _____

_____

10. To what city had Sheba fled in order to hide? _____

_____

11. What were Joab and the army preparing to do outside the city? _____

_____

12. This city was well known for what reason? _____

_____

_____

13. How did the woman of Abel reason with Joab? _____

_____

_____

14. What was Joab's response to the woman? _____

_____

_____

15. What was his request? _____

_____

_____

16. What did the woman say would be done? _____

_____

_____

17. What was the final result of the confrontation? _____

_____

_____

18. How did the woman of Abel show her wisdom? _____

_____

_____

_____

19. How was she a peacemaker? _____

_____

_____

_____

_____

20. What strength training tips can we learn from the woman of Abel?

    1.

    2.

    3.

    4.

CHAPTER 10

RIZPAH
LOVING AND PERSISTENT

LESSON TEXT /// 2 SAMUEL 21:1-14

This is the heartbreaking account of a
woman named Rizpah, who in the midst
of tragedy demonstrated such deep love and
fiery devotion that through her actions she was
able to touch the heart of a king.

*A few summers ago, while staying at the beach, I had some
time alone with my grandmother. She had come into the
kitchen to talk to me as I stood ironing clothes for the kids. I don't
recall every detail of our conversation but I do remember that
Granny talked about an inspiring letter she had received from a
dear friend. It was not uncommon for Granny to become emotional
when speaking of her family, friends, and faith and since crying is
one of the things I do best, together we were a regular tear-fest!
That afternoon we had a good cry while she taught me something
wonderful about God.*

*Gran talked to me about David: a man after God's own heart but
who struggled with sin and faced difficult trials. She told me about
a verse in the Bible that refers to God keeping David's tears in a*

bottle and how that thought has helped her many times to not feel forgotten in times of sadness. At the moment, Gran could not pinpoint the chapter and verse, and without "Google" we spent quite a bit of time flipping through our Bibles trying to find the Scripture. A year passed and while I hadn't forgotten my talk with Granny, I had failed to look further into the precious idea of God collecting tears.

Then one morning I found it! Psalm 56:8, "You number my wanderings; put my tears in Your bottle; are they not in Your book?" I wish that I could have called my grandmother and told her that I remembered our talk that afternoon and that I had found the Scripture she had told me about. She had died the previous month, never to shed another tear; and there I sat, bawling at the kitchen counter, but with a new perspective of peace in my sorrow!

God knew David. He knew David's struggles, He saw what steered David off course, He understood what brought David down. God accounted for everything that David experienced in His book; nothing was unseen or forgotten. God is not so removed from us that He doesn't know what makes us hurt! The idea of putting tears in a bottle could be a reference to a lachrymatory, which was a vase used for catching the tears of mourners in Bible times. It is a beautiful thought that God collected David's tears and kept them in HIS bottle. He had in His remembrance those things that caused David grief. As a child of God I can know with confidence that God catches my tears in His bottle too and records my afflictions and adversities in His book. While He commands my respect and obedience, He also watches over me with tenderness, compassion, and concern in times of trouble and distress.

If Granny were here I would thank her for telling me about David's tears. I would thank her for the simple conversation we had at the beach that, although at the time I didn't realize it, would so strengthen my faith and my relationship with God. She had a wonderful way of doing that.

◤ TRAILHEAD

Saul had been killed in a battle against the Philistines and David began to reign over Israel as God's chosen king. Israel was in the throes of a three year famine and David asked the Lord the reason for their suffering. The Lord told him it was because *"Saul and his bloodthirsty house"* had killed the Gibeonites. (2 Samuel 21:1)

The Lord had warned the Israelites about the consequences of disobedience. In Deuteronomy 28, from v. 15 through the end of the chapter, the Lord lists the curses that would befall their nation if they did not keep His statutes and commandments.

The Lord's anger over Saul's treatment of the Gibeonites was the result of a vow that had been made by Joshua 400 years earlier! In Joshua 9:3-27, we read the account of how Joshua was tricked by the Gibeonites into making a covenant of peace with their people and allowed them to remain in the Promised Land instead of driving them out with the other nations as God had commanded.

Saul had violated that covenant, which was an act of disobedience, regardless of his intentions. In 2 Samuel 21:2, what reason is

158

given for why Saul was attempting to destroy the Gibeonites?_____

_____

However, God remembered the covenant and atonement had to be made with the Gibeonite people in order to end the famine.

_____

 Vow making was not to be taken lightly (remember the story of Jephthah's daughter!). In Numbers 30:2, Moses explained to the Israelites that keeping a vow was a commandment from the Lord!

_____

THE TRUE STORY

AVENGING THE GIBEONITES

King David had to save his people from the famine, so he asked the Gibeonites what could be done in order for the Israelites to make atonement for the sin that had been committed against their people.

The Gibeonites did not want gold or silver, nor did they want "any man" put to death in Israel on their behalf. David assured them that whatever they requested would be done. In response, the Gibeonites demanded that seven descendants of Saul, the man who consumed and plotted against them, be delivered to them and hanged in the city of Gibeah before the Lord.

Why was the city of Gibeah significant in this deal? (1 Samuel 10:26) _____

_____

David responded to the Gibeonites with these words in 2 Samuel 21:6: *"I will give them."*

_____

It is interesting to note that in v. 7 of the text, it is noted that David spared Mephibosheth, the son of Jonathan and Saul's grandson, because of the vow of kindness he had made to him in 2 Samuel 9:1-13.

_____

So David chose seven of Saul's family members to be given into the hands of the Gibeonites: the five sons of Merab, daughter of Saul and the two sons of Rizpah, Saul's concubine. He delivered the men to the Gibeonites and they were put them to death by hanging at the beginning of the barley harvest.

_____

According to the Hebrew calendar, the barley harvest would occur in the month of Nisan, which corresponds with late March/early April.

_____

RIZPAH'S SORROW

Rizpah is first mentioned in 2 Samuel 3:7, where she is

described as being a concubine of Saul. After Saul's death, Abner, the commander of his army, declares Saul's son, Ishbosheth, king over Israel. Sometime later, Ishbosheth accused Abner of having a relationship with Rizpah. Abner is mortified over the accusation and is so upset by it that he forfeits his allegiance to Ishbosheth and joins forces with David, who has been anointed king over Judah.

In those times, a concubine was a woman living in a lawful marriage arrangement with a man, but whose status was regarded as being less than a wife. Concubines were respected, had legal rights, and their children were regarded as legitimate, although the children of the wife, or wives, were most often given preference in matters of inheritance.

Rizpah had two sons with Saul, Armoni and Mephibosheth. Saul had died and her sons had been chosen to atone the sin of their father, leaving Rizpah completely alone.

Imagine Rizpah's excruciating sorrow as a mother who lost her two sons. We simply cannot comprehend the magnitude of her suffering. Not only did her sons have to die a gruesome death, but they were also denied a proper burial and left hanging outside the city of Gibeah as a symbol of justice and restitution.

In Deuteronomy 21:22-23, it was commanded that a body not be left hanging overnight on a tree; it was defilement to the land and the one who was hanged was considered accursed of God.

RIZPAH'S EXTRAORDINARY ACTION

Her precious sons' bodies were hanging on a hill outside of
Gibeah with no indication that they would be cut down and given
back to their mother for a respectable burial. Motivated by a
mother's **love**, Rizpah took matters into her own hands. If the
leaders of her people would not see that her sons were treated
with dignity, she would take whatever measures necessary to see
that they were.

Rizpah took sackcloth and spread it on the rock at the place where
her sons and Saul's five grandsons were hanging and she guarded
over their bodies, through day and night, to protect them from the
birds and beasts of prey.

One verse describes the actions of Rizpah, but the picture that
the one verse paints is unforgettable (2 Samuel 21:10). A loving
mother, stationed at the feet of her dead sons, driving away
animals in the light of day and the darkness of night, so that they
would receive the honor they deserved.

---

*Rizpah did not attempt to cut down the bodies herself;
possibly out of submission to God, possibly due to fear,
possibly because she physically could not accomplish the task.*

RIZPAH DOES NOT GIVE UP

In v. 10, we are also given an indication of how long Rizpah kept
vigil over her sons. We are told that she remained there *"from*

the beginning of harvest until the late rains poured on them from heaven."

We know from the previous verse that the barley harvest was taking place at that time, which occurred in the spring months of March and April. "The late rains" came in the Hebrew month of Marcheshvan, which corresponds with our fall months of October and November. The Lord may have chosen an earlier time for the rain to fall, but it if the Scripture is presenting a literal time frame, then Rizpah **persevered** for six months or more at the place where her sons were killed.

How did she do it? How did she stay at her post and continue to submit herself at the feet of her sons for days, weeks, or even months? Rizpah did it because she loved her sons and she was devoted to them, which caused her to persevere in the hope that her cause would be recognized. And indeed it was.

THE KING RESPONDS

Word got back to King David about what Rizpah had done. Someone told him of Rizpah's love, devotion, and sacrifice, and it touched his heart. David's conscience was moved, not only to bury the bodies of Rizpah's two sons and the other five men, but to also properly bury the bodies of King Saul and Jonathan…all because of one woman.

The last chapter of 1 Samuel tells of the death of Saul and three of his sons, including Jonathan, in a battle against the Philistines and how the body of Saul was hung on

display by his enemies. Some men from Jabesh Gilead had gone and
removed the bodies of Saul and his sons, returned to Jabesh, burned
the bodies, and buried the bones in their land. King Saul, and David's
dear friend Jonathan, had never received a proper burial.

After the burial of these men had been completed according to the command of King David, what was God's response recorded in 2 Samuel 21:14? _____

⊱ STRENGTH TRAINING TIPS

1. **There is power in one**

    Rizpah stood alone, and through her love and persistence, changed the heart of a king. Think also of Esther, Ruth, Rahab, Tamar, Lydia, the woman at the well, and many other women in the Bible whose personal actions had a tremendous impact on God's people. If you think that what you do cannot possibly matter, read the accounts of those women and think about the trailblazers in this Bible study. One woman can do powerful things for God.

    Powerful actions don't have to be nation-saving, spy-rescuing, or vigil-making; they can come in the form of encouraging words, simple gestures, or prayers.

    For example, the words, "You're a good mom," can mean the world to a young mother who is feeling frazzled after trying to keep her children quiet through a worship service;

a note of thanks to an elderly Christian woman for her faithful example can brighten her day; the food you make for a grieving family can provide an unspoken comfort at a very difficult time; and inviting a struggling friend to a church function could change her life.

You've probably heard the saying, "God uses ordinary people for accomplishing extraordinary things!" How vividly that concept shines through the life of Rizpah and the other trailblazers in this study! One woman CAN make a difference—not because she is extraordinary in and of herself—but because she serves an extraordinary God!

How has one person, one word, or one gesture had a profound impact on your life? _____

_____

_____

What can you do to make a difference in someone's life?

_____

_____

_____

Not only does this one woman's amazing life continue to influence from the pages of the Bible, but also through the avenue of poetry from the pens of literary giants. Read the poems entitled, "Rizpah" by Alfred Lord Tennyson and "Mother O'Mine" by Rudyard Kipling and discover how her account touched the lives of these two men.

---

2. **Take a stand for what is right and what is just (even when no one else will) and you will receive the blessing of your King**

Rizpah made certain that her sons were given a proper burial, even though it meant she stood alone...for months...in harrowing conditions. She did it because she loved them, and it was not right for them to be treated so indignantly. In the end, Rizpah was blessed for her actions.

I'm reminded of the story we read in Daniel 1. It was during the time of the Babylonian captivity and Daniel had been chosen among others to serve in King Nebuchadnezzar's palace. It had been commanded that the chosen men be given a daily provision of the king's food and wine, but Daniel refused. It may have been that Daniel was concerned that the food offered would not meet the requirements of Mosaic Law in how it was prepared or whether it came from a clean animal; or the food and drink may have been dedicated to Babylonian idols which was customary in that time. Whatever the reason, eating the food and drinking the wine violated Daniel's conscience and he took a stand for what was right.

Daniel asked that he and his friends, Shadrach, Meshach, and Abed-Nego, be given only vegetables and water for a period of ten days. At the end of that time, their physical appearances could be examined and compared to the other men. In v. 15, we read what happened:

"And at the end of ten days their features appeared better and fatter in flesh than all the young men who at the portion of the king's delicacies."

But that wasn't all! Daniel and his friends were further blessed by God:

"As for these four young men, God gave them knowledge and skill in all literature and wisdom; and Daniel had understanding in all visions and dreams." (Daniel 1:17)

God rewards those who diligently seek Him (Hebrews 11:6) and He blesses those who are righteous (Psalm 5:12).

Read Luke 11:28 and James 1:25. According to these verses, who will be blessed by God? _____

_____

In what ways can you take a stand for what is right? _____

_____

_____

Read Daniel 1:8 and Daniel 10:12. What does it mean that Daniel "purposed in his heart" and "set his heart to understand?" How did this help Daniel when it came to making the right choices? _____

_____

_____

3. **Demonstrate persistent determination in prayer**

Just as Rizpah never gave up on her appeal to the king, so we should not give up on our appeals to our King. David heard of Rizpah's persistence and responded. How much more will God, our Heavenly Father, respond to His children?

In Luke 18:1-7, Jesus told His disciples a parable about not losing heart in their prayers. He described a widow in a city who cried out to the judge for justice from her adversaries. The judge did not fear God nor did he have respect for others, and he was pestered by the widow continually for a period of time. Finally, the judge avenged her just because he was tired of being troubled by her request. Jesus said, in v. 7, *"And shall God not avenge His own elect who cry out day and night to Him, though He bears long with them?"*

In essence, Jesus was asking His disciples, if the unjust judge would grant the request of the widow, will God not answer the prayers of His own people who cry out to Him day and night? Could Jesus have been thinking about Rizpah?

In Matthew 7:7, Jesus said *"Ask, and it will be given to you; seek, and you will find; knock, and it will be opened to you."* The verbs ask, seek, and knock are expressed in the present active imperative form. In other words, "keep on asking, keep on seeking, and keep on knocking."

Never quit praying; God will answer. He is concerned about you and He is collecting your tears.

Does God always give us what we ask? _____

_____

_____

_____

How do we grow stronger through persistence in prayer? __

_____

_____

_____

4. **Love faithfully and sacrificially**

I think of Rizpah when I read 1 Corinthians 13. When I read the words in v. 4, *"love suffers long,"* I visualize Rizpah at the feet of her sons driving away the animals and birds of prey. When I read in v. 7 that, love *"bears all things, believes all things, hopes all things, endures all things,"* I imagine Rizpah battling hunger, exhaustion, and fear as she pursued justice for her sons. In v. 8, when Paul writes, *"Love never fails,"* I picture Rizpah enduring the ridicule of others, ignoring her own needs, and suffering through her grief until David took notice.

Love is characterized by devotion. Love is faithful. This is kind of love that God has for us, the kind of love that never leaves.

Nothing could separate Rizpah from the vigil she held by the bodies of her sons and the Bible tells us that nothing can separate us from the love of God.

"Who shall separate us from the love of Christ? Shall tribulation, or distress, or persecution, or famine, or nakedness, or peril, or sword? As it is written: 'for Your sake we are killed all day long; we are accounted as sheep for the slaughter.' Yet in all these things we are more than conquerors through Him who loved us. For I am persuaded that neither death nor life, nor angels nor principalities nor powers, nor things present nor things to come, nor height nor depth, nor any other created thing, shall be able to separate us from the love of God which is in Christ Jesus our Lord" (Romans 8:35-39).

Who do you love faithfully? _____

_____

In what ways do you sacrifice for those you love? _____

_____

_____

How are you demonstrating your devotion to them? _____

_____

_____

_____

 "Love never fails." 1 Corinthians 13:8a

◣TRAILMARKERS

1. Where do we read the account of Rizpah in the Bible? ____

    _____

2. Who is the king of Israel at this time? _____

    _____

3. What hardship is the Israelite nation experiencing? _____

    _____

4. How long had it been going on? _____

    _____

5. What was the cause? _____

    _____

6. What vow had Joshua taken with the Gibeonites 400 years earlier? _____

    _____

    _____

7. What had to be done in order to end God's chastisement of Israel? _____

_____

_____

_____

8. What was the demand made by the Gibeonites? _____

_____

_____

_____

9. Who was handed over to the Gibeonites? _____

_____

_____

_____

_____

10. What was Rizpah's connection to King Saul? _____

_____

_____

11. Following their deaths, what injustice was dealt to the sons of Rizpah? _____

_____

_____

12. What was Rizpah's reaction? _____

_____

_____

_____

13. How long did Rizpah keep a vigil? _____

_____

14. What motivated Rizpah to do what she did? _____
_____

15. What was the result of her actions? _____
_____
_____
_____

16. Furthermore, what did King David "make right" at this
time? _____
_____

17. What was God's response? _____
_____
_____

18. What does Rizpah teach us about love? _____
_____
_____
_____

19. What does she teach us about persevering? _____
_____
_____
_____

20. What strength training tips can we learn from Rizpah?

1.

2.

3.

4.

CHAPTER 11

THE SHUNAMMITE WOMAN

KIND AND FAITHFUL

LESSON TEXT /// 2 KINGS 4:8-37

The woman from Shunem is memorialized in the Bible for the unconditional kindness she extended to a man of God, her ability to be content with what she had been given, and her unwavering faith through the darkest hour of her life.

My kids are pretty fearless. They like fast amusement park rides, jellyfish stings don't keep them out of the ocean, and there is no trace of acrophobia in their little bodies. They eat sushi.

A few years ago, Evie and Kate rappelled down Copperhead Cliff at Fall Creek Falls State Park. Our family had been indoor rock-climbing before, but that was their first "real life" experience. They loved it! In fact, as Kate was rappelling to the bottom of the cliff, you could hear her yelling, "Weeeeeeeee" every time she pushed herself away from the rocks.

The next weekend, we went rock-climbing again and Briggs made his first ascent. He did fantastic!

While my kids were climbing up and rappelling down the rock walls, I found myself closely watching their belayers. The jobs of the belayer are to pull the slack through a belay device as the climber goes up the wall, "catch" the climber if they fall, and control the descent of the climber back to the ground. As the belayer, the safety of the climber is in your hands! As the climber, you have to have complete faith in the ability of your belayer.

Faith. I like it defined this way: "having a confident belief and a confident hope, which motivate you to take action." As Christians, our belief is in God our Father; our hope is for eternal life with Him in Heaven. That belief and that hope, together, incite our obedience to His Will, which is revealed to us in the Bible.

I read an article once about a missionary named John Paton who translated the Bible for islanders of the South Sea in the latter part of the 19th century. He had not been able to find a word in their vocabulary for the concept of believing, trusting, or having faith. One day, while he was in his hut translating, a native came running in and sat down in a chair, utterly exhausted. He said to Paton, "It is so good to rest my whole weight in this chair". And there it was! John Paton had his word for faith: "resting your whole weight on God". I like this definition too.

I think of Evie, Kate, and Briggs literally "resting their whole weight" on me or Sam as we belayed for them while they climbed to the top of the rock walls. This is a wonderful lesson for the Christian!

Is there anything more assuring than knowing that as we face challenges daily, as we struggle to meet our goals, as we climb and fall over obstacles in our lives; we can rest our whole weight on God, knowing that He is holding our rope, and He will keep us safe.

◤ TRAILHEAD

The Israelites had been divided into two separate kingdoms: the Northern Kingdom of Israel and the Southern Kingdom of Judah. At that time, God was speaking through prophets as His people continued down the road of sin that would ultimately lead to their captivity.

The Northern Kingdom of Israel was comprised of ten of the Israelite tribes, excluding Judah and Benjamin, who were part of the Southern Kingdom of Judah.

Israel was under the leadership of King Jehoram, who was an evil king, and Jehoshaphat was king over Judah, a good king but with a heart that was not completely turned to God. Elisha was serving as God's prophet in Israel following his predecessor, Elijah.

How was Elijah taken to Heaven? (2 Kings 2:11) _____

Elisha traveled throughout the kingdom ministering to the people and serving the Lord.

The prophets preached a message of repentance, warned the people about the consequences of falling away from God, and predicted events that would occur in the future. Paul describes the role of a prophet in the New Testament in 1 Corinthians 14:3. For what three purposes does a prophet speak?

_____, _____,

_____

_____

☛THE TRUE STORY

ELISHA, A TRAVELING PROPHET

Elisha walked all throughout the kingdom of Israel and preached to the people as God's spokesman. In 2 Kings 2, we are told that Elisha traveled from Samaria, to Gilgal, to Bethel, to Mount Carmel, and then returned to Samaria, working for God in each place along his route.

In 2 Kings 4:8, Elisha has come to the city of Shunem, a regular place for him to stop on journeys to Mount Carmel.

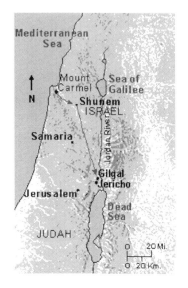

Mount Carmel must have been a place for religious gatherings, as later in the story (v. 23) we find that might people would go there at the time of the New Moon or the Sabbath, to make peace offerings or burnt offerings (Numbers 10:10).

A HOSPITABLE WOMAN

In Shunem, there was a certain woman who took notice of Elisha as he passed through her city. She is described as being "notable," which indicates that she may have been a woman of some influence, well respected in her community, or possibly even wealthy. When she saw Elisha, she persuaded him to stop at her home and eat. Over time it happened that whenever he passed through Shunem, he would go to her home for a meal.

The word persuaded *in 2 Kings 4:8, is translated from the Hebrew word* chazaq *meaning "to fasten upon" or "to seize." I picture the Shunammite woman taking Elisha by the arm and insisting that he stop and have something to eat! Have you ever known a woman like that? You aren't going to leave her house without a full stomach or food to take home with you!*

The Shunammite woman went further in showing Elisha hospitality when she approached her husband with an idea she had:

"Look now, I know that this is a holy man of God, who passes by us regularly. Please, let us make a small upper room on the wall; and let us put a bed for him there, and a table, and a chair and a lampstand; so it will be, whenever he comes to us, he can turn in there" (2 Kings 4:9-10).

She wanted to make a guest room for Elisha! Her husband must have agreed, because in v. 11, Elisha is in the upper room, resting on the bed.

What a blessing this woman was to Elisha. He knew that no matter how difficult his journey, there was a hot meal, a warm bed, and a **kind** friend waiting for him in Shunem.

Read Matthew 25:31-40 and discover who Jesus says will inherit the kingdom of God. Sounds very much like the Shunammite woman!

ELISHA'S OFFER

Elisha had a servant named Gehazi. As he rested in his upper room at the home of the Shunammite woman, he asked his servant to call the woman and give her a message. Elisha wanted Gehazi to find out how he could repay her for all of the kindness she had shown to him. He even offered to speak to the king or to the commander of the army on her behalf. The woman could ask for anything she wanted and Elisha would deliver.

The Shunammite woman stood before Gehazi as he conveyed the offer of his master. She simply answered, *"I dwell among my people."*

Those five words speak volumes about her character. She didn't want or need anything from Elisha. She lived among her people and was content with what she had. However, Gehazi knew there was more to her story, she did have an unspoken desire, and he would share that with his master.

"What then is to be done for her?" Elisha asked when Gehazi told him about his conversation with the woman. Gehazi answered, *"Actually, she has no son, and her husband is old."*

"Call her," Elisha requested.

The woman came and stood in the doorway of Elisha's guest room and he said to her, *"About this time next year, you shall embrace a son."*

The woman cried out, *"No, my lord. Man of God, do not lie to your maidservant!"*

She could not bear the burden of renewed hope for something she knew she could never have. She had found contentment in her life and begged him not to promise something she had conditioned her heart to live without.

What happened in 2 Kings 4:17? _____

_____

_____

The Shunammite woman was blessed...

A TRAGEDY

...and the little boy grew! One day, while his father was out with the reapers, the child came to him crying out, *"My head, my head!"* His father had one of his servants carry the boy to his mother. The woman held him in her lap until noon and then, while in her arms, her young son died.

From a medical standpoint, this may have been a massive head injury resulting in internal bleeding. Often times, these patients are alert and oriented after the initial injury, but as bleeding on the brain continues unseen, the patient shows signs of decreased level of consciousness and, without intervention, death can occur. Today, we have emergency surgery available in these situations, but in Old Testament time there was nothing that could be done except to wait for the inevitable.

She took him to the guest room she had made for Elisha and laid his body on the bed, shut the door, and went out.

She knew what she had to do.

A WOMAN'S RESOLVE

The Shunammite woman called her husband and asked that he send her one of their young male servants and a donkey. She explained to him that she had to run to the man of God and then come back.

"Why are you going to see him today?" her husband asked. *"It is neither the New Moon nor the Sabbath."*

And she said, *"It is well."*

What unbelievable **faith**! Her son is dead, she is embarking on an emergency mission to find Elisha, and yet she tells her husband, "Everything is okay." In fact, she doesn't even mention the death of their son; she is certain that what has happened can be changed!

 Remember: Faith is a confident belief and a confident hope that motivate us to take action!

Is it possible that the Shunammite woman had heard the news about how Elisha's predecessor, Elijah, had healed the son of a widow? (1 Kings 17:17-24)

She saddled a donkey and told the servant, *"Drive, and go forward; do not slacken the pace for me unless I tell you."* Then they set out in the direction of Mount Carmel to find the man of God.

Just as Deborah's presence with Barak and the Israelite army on Mount Tabor represented a tangible form of God's presence, so Elisha represented a physical means of accessing God's miraculous power for the healing of her son. Getting to Elisha meant getting to God.

Elisha saw her coming from a distance and sent his servant to go meet her. He told Gehazi to inquire, *"Is it well with you? Is it well with your husband? Is it well with the child?"* and to all of these questions the woman answered, *"It is well."*

But she needed Elisha. She caught up to him and took hold of his feet. Gehazi tried to push her away, but Elisha stopped him because he recognized that her soul was in such deep distress and the Lord had not revealed to him what had happened to her son.

The woman, in anguish, admonished Elisha saying, *"Did I ask you to give me a son? Didn't I say, 'Do not deceive me?'"* She wanted to know why Elisha would promise to give her something so precious only to take it away.

Elisha instructed Gehazi to take his staff, go with the woman to her home, not to talk to anyone along the way, and then lay the staff on the face of the child. This was not going to suffice for the Shunammite woman. She told Elisha, *"As the Lord lives, and as your soul lives, I will not leave you."*

So Elisha went.

THE HAPPY ENDING

Gehazi ran ahead and tried laying the staff on the face of the child, but nothing happened. He returned to Elisha and the woman and told them that the child had not awakened. Elisha entered his guest room and saw the child lying dead on his bed. He shut the door and prayed.

Then he walked over to the child and lay down on top of him. He stretched himself out over the child: mouth on mouth, eyes on eyes, hands on hands; and the flesh of the child became warm.

Notice in vv. 33-35, the repetitious use of the word "and". This is a literary technique known as "polysyndeton." This technique uses conjunctions to slow down or speed up the rhythm of the text and to provide emphasis on each item in a list. In this case it gives importance to each separate action of Elisha and builds up to the dramatic conclusion. It is used frequently throughout Scripture (Genesis 7:22-24, Haggai 1:11, 1 Corinthians 13:1-3).

Elisha walked back and forth in the house, then returned and stretched himself on top of the child again. The boy sneezed seven times....and opened his eyes!

Seven is the number of perfection. Consider how it is used in the Bible: seven days of creation, seven animals of sacrifice on the ark, seven years of labor by Jacob for Leah and seven more years for Rachel, seven dips in the water by Naaman, seven things the Lord hates, forgiveness seventy-times-seven, seven churches in Revelation, and there are many other examples.

A WOMAN'S GRATITUDE

Elisha sent Gehazi to bring the Shunammite woman to the room. When she came, Elisha said, *"Pick up your son."*

She entered the room, but instead of rushing to her son's side, she fell at the feet of Elisha and bowed to the ground. Elisha, by the power of God, had restored her son's life, and the woman expressed her thankfulness first; then, she lifted her precious son into her arms.

STRENGTH TRAINING TIPS

1.   **Kindness opens the door for more blessings**

I once read that kindness is the most difficult thing to get rid of, because when you give it away...it will keep coming back!

It is not that we should be kind to others with the expectation that we will get something in return, but rather, because of the joy that comes in the giving.

Luke reminds us of Jesus' words in Acts 20:35, *"It is more blessed to give than to receive."* God is pleased when we do good to others and share what we have (Hebrews 13:16), and He loves a cheerful giver (2 Corinthians 9:7).

We show kindness to others because it pleases God, and if that is our motivation...then the blessings will follow!

"Give and it will be given to you: good measure, pressed down, shaken together, and running over will be put into your bosom. For with the same measure that you use, it will be measured back to you" (Luke 6:38).

"There is one who scatters, yet increases more; and there is one who withholds more than is right, but it leads to poverty. The generous soul will be made rich, and he who waters will also be watered himself" (Proverbs 11:24-25).

Just days before His crucifixion, Jesus spoke to His disciples on the Mount of Olives. On that occasion, He gave them an illustration of the Judgment when the Son of Man will gather all the nations and separate them to the

His right and left. Then the King will declare who will inherit the kingdom and who will be sent into the everlasting fire.

Read Matthew 25:31-46. What had the righteous done to inherit the kingdom? _____

_____

_____

God takes kindness personally. Read v. 40 again in Matthew 25, and then read Proverbs 19:17. When we help others, to whom are we actually showing kindness? _____

_____

_____

In the second part of Proverbs 19:17, what will the Lord do for those who lend to the poor? _____

_____

_____

2.   **When contentment is paired with godliness, there will be great gain**

This is what Paul told Timothy in 1 Timothy 6:6, and then went on to explain the dangers of desiring wealth and loving money.

To be content is to be happy with what you have; and to be godly is to be deeply committed to your faith, conforming to the laws and wishes of God. When you put these two righteous characteristics together, much good will come.

The Shunammite woman demonstrated contentment and godliness, first, when she declined Elisha's offer to repay her kindness by saying *"I dwell among my own people."* She had found peace in her life even though it was down a road that she might not have chosen. She had no children, and in the emotional responses she gave, in 2 Kings 4:16, 28, it is clear that a child was something she had desperately wanted. However, despite the desires of her heart, she had discovered contentment and provided faithful service to God's prophet, Elisha, and expected nothing in return.

Then, God made her family grow.

We see more powerful evidence of the Shunammite woman's contentment and godliness in the three small words she repeated twice:

"It is well."

She spoke those words following an unimaginable tragedy: the death of her son. When she called her husband to help her prepare to find Elisha, she told him nothing about what had happened, just that she needed to get to the man of God; and when questioned about the reason, she simply answered, *"It is well."*

When met by Elisha's servant Gehazi along the road and he asked about her, her husband, and their child, she replied only with the words, *"It is well."*

How is it that the Shunammite woman could say, *"It is well."* As her son lay motionless in his bed, how could she believe that everything was *"well?"* It was because of her spirit of contentment and the deep faith she had that Elisha, through the power of God, would take care of everything. As

Christians today, when we "rest our whole weight" on God, we can be sure that He will take care of us, too. Like the Shunammite woman, we can say, *"It is well."*

At what point in our lives should we expect to find contentment? (Read the words of Paul in Philippians 4:11). _____

_____

How is godliness demonstrated? _____

_____

_____

3. **In our times of trouble we need to "get to God" and lay our problems down at His feet**

The Shunammite woman knew that she needed to get to Elisha, and she would stop at nothing to get there, because it was through him that she had direct contact to Almighty God. She believed that Elisha, through the power of God, could restore her son.

Today, we don't have to go to anyone else in order to "get to God"; we have direct access to Him through His Son, Jesus Christ! However, we should strive to have the mindset of the Shunammite woman: she knew who could help her, she sought him out, and she fell at his feet.

She encountered obstacles: her questioning husband, a distance to be traveled, the intervening Gehazi; but the Shunammite woman was unhindered. Today we can "get to God" through prayer at any time and for any reason; and there is nothing that stands in our way unless it is our own lack of faith.

"Cast your burden on the Lord, and He shall sustain you; He shall never permit the righteous to be moved" (Psalm 55:22).

What obstacles might prevent someone from being able to "get to God" today? _____

_____

Think of your greatest hindrance when it comes to prayer. What can you do to help overcome that obstacle? _____

_____

_____

Read Psalm 34:15-17 and 145:18-19. What will God do when we come to Him with our troubles? _____

_____

_____

Organize a women's prayer devotional for a group of your friends. Plan a time for all of you to come together and lift each other up in prayer. You will all be edified and strengthened; and God will be glorified.

---

4.   **Remember to say "thank you"**

"And one of them, when he saw that he was healed, returned, and with a loud voice glorified God, and fell down on his face at His feet, giving Him thanks. And he was a Samaritan. So Jesus answered and said, 'Were there not ten cleansed? But where are the nine? Were there not

any found who returned to give glory to God except this foreigner?' And He said to him, 'Arise, go your way. Your faith has made you well'" (Luke 17:15-19).

The account of the ten lepers is one that we share with children at a young age to teach them the importance of being thankful. Only one of the ten lepers healed by Jesus returned to show his gratitude and Jesus commended him.

Even Jesus thanked God for hearing and answering His prayer. When His friend Lazarus had died, Jesus came and stood outside the tomb. He lifted up His eyes and spoke to God saying, *"Father, I thank You that You have heard Me"* (John 11:41).

After Elisha restored the Shunammite Woman's son and she was brought back into the room, the very first thing she did was fall at the feet of Elisha in humble thanksgiving. She was faithful, she received a blessing, and she expressed her thankfulness.

Christians should have a spirit of gratitude continually (Hebrews 13:15) because of God's grace, but we cannot forget to specifically thank God for answering our prayers and to glorify Him for our blessings.

Why is it important to say "thank you"? What do those words truly mean? _____

_____

_____

How do you express your thanks to others? _____

_____

How can you continually show gratitude to God? _____

_____

_____

We read in 1 Thessalonians 5:17, we should "pray without ceasing"; speak to God continually, throughout the day. When you're suddenly faced with a problem, a choice, a blessing, or an opportunity; get in the habit of involving God right then, in prayer. "Get to God" not only when it comes to the big things, but also with the little things!

"And let us not grow weary while doing good, for in due season we shall reap if we do not lose heart. Therefore, as we have opportunity, let us do good to all, especially to those who are of the household of faith." Galatians 6:9-10

TRAILMARKERS

1.   Where do we find the account of the Shunammite woman in the Bible? _____

_____

2.   The Israelites were divided into the Northern Kingdom of _____ and the Southern Kingdom of

_____.

3. Who is Elisha? _____
   _____

4. In what city would Elisha stop on his way to Mount Carmel?
   _____
   _____

5. What is meant by "notable" when the Scripture describes
   the Shunammite woman? _____
   _____
   _____

6. What did the Shunammite woman do for Elisha? _____
   _____
   _____
   _____

7. Who is Gehazi? _____
   _____

8. What did Elisha want his servant to find out for him? _____
   _____
   _____
   _____

9. What does the woman mean when she tells Elisha, "I dwell
   among my own people"? _____
   _____
   _____
   _____

10. What does Gehazi know about the Shunammite woman
    that he reveals to Elisha? _____
    _____

11. What does Elisha promise the woman? _____

12. What is her response? _____

13. How was the Shunammite woman blessed? _____

14. What tragedy occurred in the woman's life a short time later? _____

15. What did the woman say to her husband and to Gehazi that reflects her faith in God? _____

16. What did she say to Elisha that reflects her persistence? __

17. What did the woman do first upon entering her child's room after the miracle? _____

18. How did the Shunammite woman demonstrate kindness? _

_____

_____

19.   How did she demonstrate faithfulness? _____

_____

_____

_____

_____

_____

20.   What strength training tips can we learn from the Shunammite woman?

    1.

    2.

    3.

    4.

CHAPTER 12

HULDAH
RESPECTED AND READY

LESSON TEXT /// 2 KINGS 22:1-20
AND 2 CHRONICLES 34-35

A good king, reigning over an evil kingdom on the brink of doom, requested to hear the words of the Lord for direction and hope, and so his trusted advisors sent for the prophetess Huldah. God needed her to boldly convey a fateful message to the king, and when that time came...she was ready.

"She is a 'ministering angel' without any exaggeration in these hospitals, and as her slender form glides quietly along each corridor, every poor fellow's face softens with gratitude at the sight of her. When all the medical officers have retired for the night and silence and darkness have settled down upon those miles of prostrate sick, she may be observed alone, with a little lamp in her hand, making her solitary rounds."

Those words were printed in the British newspaper, The Times, in reference to Florence Nightingale, a woman remembered today as the founder of modern nursing. During the Crimean War, she became known as "The Lady of the Lamp," because she would make her hospital rounds at night, carrying a small lantern and caring for wounded soldiers.

Florence Nightingale made it her mission in life to serve the hurting and the dying. She was not of the sick, but she was sent to work in hospitals **among** the sick to provide them with help and hope. She indeed was a "Lady of the Lamp": A light shining in the darkness.

We are to be a separate people, knowing that we do not belong to this world or live according to its values. It is equally important to remember that we have been given a command to go into the world to preach the Gospel. As Florence Nightingale was sent **into** hospitals to care for the sick, we have been sent **into** the world to save the lost.

I want to be a "Lady of the Lamp." I want to be a light shining in the darkness. I want to be someone who brings hope to the hurting. I want to be close enough to the sick that they can see the light reflecting on my face and see the love of Christ. I want to be in situations where I can take a stand for what is right. I want the warmth and brightness of my lamp to draw people closer to God. I want to be recognized in the world by my light. I want to shine so that people know where to find me and be close enough for them to reach out and touch me. I want others to see me coming and know that I am someone who can offer help.

I imagine Florence Nightingale walking down a dark hall of the hospital with her lamp, caring for the sick lined up along the walls. I picture a wounded man at the end of hall watching the little flicker of light from her lamp and knowing that help was coming, yearning for the touch of the nurse. I pray that God will make me a "Lady of the Lamp;" that He will help me shine as I go out into this world and instill within me the sincere and loving desire to bring others out.

◤TRAILHEAD

Israel had forgotten God. Under the leadership of King Manasseh, the Southern Kingdom of Judah had fallen into complete apostasy. For the fifty-five years of his reign, Manasseh promoted sinful practices and drew the hearts of the people away from the Lord. He rebuilt the high places for pagan worship, raised up altars for Baal and other false gods, placed idols in the temple, made his son "pass through the fire," practiced soothsaying, used witchcraft, consulted spiritists and mediums, and shed much innocent blood "till he had filled Jerusalem from one end to another" (2 Kings 21:2-26). Manasseh was a very wicked king.

The term, "pass through the fire," could either refer to actual human sacrifice or, as is the case this text, the ritualistic consecration of a child to Molech, an idol of the Ammonites, by passing between two great fires. In 2 Kings 21:6, it says that the king made "his son pass through the fire" and in v. 18 of that same chapter, his son, Amon, was still alive and assumed the throne at age twenty-two.

After Manasseh's death, his son Amon reigned in his place. He followed in his father's evil footsteps and "walked in all the ways that his father had walked" (2 Kings 21:21). Amon was killed in his own home by some of his servants, and had ruled over Judah for only two years.

The people of the land took Amon's son Josiah and made him king. He would be the last good king to rule over Judah and through him there was a final opportunity for the nation to return to God. After his death, there would be four other kings to rule before the nation fell into Babylonian captivity, and all who followed Josiah to the throne were evil.

How old was Josiah when he became king? (2 Kings 22:1). _____

The Bible says, in 2 Kings 22:2, that Josiah *"did what was right in the sight of the Lord, and walked in all the ways of his father David; he did not turn aside to the right hand or to the left."*

Josiah was the son of Amon and the grandson of Manasseh, both wicked kings throughout their reigns, but his mother was named Jedidah, meaning "Beloved of the Lord." It could be that Josiah's faith was the result of a godly mother as well as the influence of the high priest Hilkiah.

God continued to use men and women as His messengers to the people, warning them of the destruction they would face and pleading with them to repent. The prophets Zephaniah and Jeremiah, and the prophetess Huldah, lived during the reign of Josiah.

⯈THE TRUE STORY

GOOD KING, BAD KINGDOM

King Josiah brought righteousness back to the throne in Judah. In the short time that had passed since his birth, the young king had developed a spirit of love and faithfulness to God, but his kingdom, however, had not. Through the worship of idols, heathen religious practices, corrupt behavior, and self-centered living, the Israelites had completely rejected God.

At age sixteen, the eighth year of his reign, Josiah began to seek the God of his father David and four years later he initiated a reform that his kingdom had not seen since the days of Hezekiah, Josiah's great-grandfather. He purged Judah and Jerusalem of the high places, the altars, the wooden images, the carved images, and the molded images. He not only removed the images, he beat them down into dust and scattered them over the graves of those who sacrificed to them! He watched them break down the altars to the Baals, and he burned the bones of the priests on their altars to the false gods.

King Josiah returned to Jerusalem after eliminating pagan symbols and idol worship throughout all the land of Israel.

LOST AND FOUND

When Josiah was in his eighteenth year as king, at age twenty-six, he sent three men to begin the work of repairing of the temple: Shaphan, the scribe, Maaseiah, the governor of the city, and Joah, the recorder. He instructed them to go to Hilkiah, the high priest, and have him count the money in the temple that the doorkeepers had gathered from the people.

The Israelites brought portions of their money to the temple, according to 2 Kings 22:4, which was collected by the priests who stood at the door. By the order of King Johoash (also called Joash), a former "good" ruler of Judah, that money was to be used for repairing the damages of the temple.

King Josiah further ordered that the money be delivered into the hands of the temple overseers and for it to be used to pay carpenters, builders, and masons so that the house of the Lord could be fully repaired.

Somewhere, in the middle of all of the fixing up, cleaning out, and reorganizing of the temple, Hilkiah made an astounding discovery! He called for Shaphan and said to him,

"I have found the Book of the Law in the house of the Lord."

This was commonly believed to have been the book of Deuteronomy, but some speculate that it could have been the first five books of the Bible written by Moses. The Torah

(Hebrew) and the Pentateuch (Greek), both refer to the first five books of the Bible.

Shaphan took the book from Hilkiah and read it, then carried it to the king.

After Shaphan reported that the temple repairs were underway, he explained that a book had been found in the process, and then read it out loud to the king.

When King Josiah heard the words of the Law, he tore his clothes.

In the Bible, the custom of tearing one's clothing was a physical expression of grief or dismay (Genesis 37:29, Job 1:20), and also symbolized the removal of one's authority (1 Samuel 15:27-28, Acts 14:11-15). In reference to this custom, what command did the Lord give the Israelites through his prophet Joel? (Joel 2:13). _____

"INQUIRE OF THE LORD"

King Josiah had to hear the words of the Lord. He knew the Lord was angry with the people because of their disobedience, but what would that mean for the future of the nation? Josiah sent Hilkiah, Shaphan, Ahikam (Shaphan's son), Achbor (or Abdon), and Asaiah to find out information from one of God's prophets.

The men went to speak to the prophetess Huldah.

Huldah was the wife of a man named Shallum, the keeper of the wardrobe. She lived in Jerusalem in the Second Quarter.

What type of person might God have chosen to speak His words to the people? Someone wise...yes; someone prayerful...yes; someone knowledgeable of the Law...yes; someone **respected** among the people...most certainly. Huldah must have been a woman well known and trusted by the king and his advisors. God chose her, because of who she was, to be His messenger.

 Huldah may have been the aunt of Jeremiah as they were contemporaries and he refers to his uncle "Shallum" several times in Jeremiah 32.

"INQUIRE OF THE LORD"

Huldah was **ready** with a direct message from God for the five men to take back to King Josiah (2 Kings 22:15-20 and 2 Chronicles 34:23-28). The Lord said that He would indeed bring calamity on Judah and its inhabitants with all of the curses in the book that had been read to the king because of their disobedience!

 Read Deuteronomy 28 to find out why the Israelites had reason to be very afraid!

The Lord went on to say that because of Josiah's tender heart and because he had humbled himself before God when he heard the words of the Law, He would not bring about the affliction on Judah until after Josiah's death.

*It is interesting that Josiah is addressed as a "man" by the Lord through Huldah, in 2 Kings 22:15 and 2 Chronicles 34:23 ("Tell the **man** who sent you to me..."); but when Huldah addresses Josiah, she respectfully refers to him as "king", in 2 Kings 22:18 and 2 Chronicles 34:26 ("But as for the **king** of Judah, who sent you to inquire of the Lord...")*

As a result of Huldah's prophecy, Josiah took the following actions:

- Read the Book of the Law to the inhabitants of the land
- Made a covenant with God to keep His commandments
- Removed all abominations from the land
- Required that the Israelites serve the Lord diligently
- Reinstituted the Feast of the Passover

"Now before him there was no king like him, who turned to the Lord with all his heart, with all his soul, with all his might, according to all the Law of Moses; nor after him did any arise like him" (2 Kings 23:25).

Whatever obligations Huldah had in her day-to-day life, she was available and ready for God to use her in a mighty way. She is forever remembered for being the woman who courageously spoke to a king and shared an unforgettable proclamation from God that foretold the impending collapse of a nation but extended mercy to an obedient king with a good heart.

⚏ STRENGTH TRAINING TIPS

1.   **Have a reputation for being a "woman of God"**

When King Josiah sent out his men to "inquire of the Lord" regarding the Book of the Law that had been found, they went to Huldah. There were other prophets living at that time, so why did they choose Huldah to speak the words of the Lord to their king? She had to have been known, she had to have been respected, and she had to have been faithful; but also, she had to have been able to present the truth to King Josiah in a kind and tenderhearted way. She was preceded by her reputation!

I hope that when people have spiritual questions they need answered, my name comes to mind as someone they can come to for help; someone who will tell them the truth, in love. I want to have that type of reputation: a woman of God, who is respected, faithful, and kind. I want to be a "Lady of the Lamp!"

In Proverbs 22:1 and Ecclesiastes 7:1, what does the Bible say is better than *"great riches"* and *"precious ointment"*? _____

When Paul wrote his letter to the church at Philippi, he told them that their conduct should be worthy of the Gospel of Christ, so that whether he was with them or away from them, he would hear of their unity and that they were working together for the faith of the Gospel (Philippians 1:27). Their conduct would determine their reputation.

How do you develop a reputation for being a "woman of God?" _____

_____

_____

Do you know someone who you would describe as a "woman of God?" What is it about her that causes you to characterize her in such a way? _____

_____

_____

"Live in such a way that if someone spoke badly of you, nobody would believe it."

---

2.   Share the Word of God regardless of the reaction you might get

Huldah had a grave message to deliver to King Josiah and she had no idea how that message would be received. She knew the writings of the Law and God had revealed to her the plans He had for Judah, but she could not be sure how the king would respond to her words. Even so, Huldah stood before Josiah and spoke honestly to him about the fate of the kingdom.

Huldah's situation makes me think of the Apostle Paul. At a time when Christians were being persecuted and to speak about Jesus was a crime, Paul earnestly shared the message of the Gospel. In Acts 18:5, we find that

Paul was *"compelled by the Spirit and testified to the Jews that Jesus is the Christ."* He was met with opposition and blasphemy, but that didn't stop Paul! He never stopped spreading the good news about Jesus until the day his life ended in Rome. In the same way, the Word of God should compel us to take action, regardless of the possible reactions!

The word compelled is translated from the Greek work *ouvexw*, which means "to constrain," meaning to be forced, or driven, to take action. It is the same word Paul used in 2 Corinthians 5:14 (emp. added), when he wrote, *"For the love of Christ **compels** us."* Paul felt a strong need—an urgency—to tell other people about the salvation found in Jesus. He even endured suffering for the cause of Christ (2 Corinthians 11:22-28).

Our love for Christ and the hope we have for Heaven because of His life, death, and resurrection should motivate us to *"go into all the world and preach the gospel to every creature"* (Mark 16:15).

In Luke 9:1-6, we read where Jesus sent out His twelve apostles to preach the kingdom of God and heal the sick. What did He tell them to do if their message was not received in a certain place (v. 5)? _____

_____

_____

What would be different about your daily life if you felt "compelled" or "constrained," like Paul, to share the Word of God? _____

_____

_____

3.   **Give an answer with meekness and fear**

Huldah was the right person for the task that was at
hand: to tell a good king that the curses mentioned in
the Book of the Law would come to pass as a result of
the wickedness of God's people. Her message conveyed
the words of the Lord and the anger He felt toward the
disobedient kingdom, but it also communicated hope and
peace to Josiah because of his faithfulness.

The way that Huldah presented the truth must have had an
impact on Josiah, because he set into action a restoration
movement that the inhabitants of the land had never
before experienced. We learn from Huldah that how you
say something can be just as important as what you say.

In 1 Peter 3:15, the Bible says, _"But sanctify the Lord God
in your hearts, and always be ready to give a defense to
everyone who asks you a reason for the hope that is in you,
with meekness and fear."_

In the previous Strength Training Tip, we discussed sharing
the Word of God regardless of the reaction you might get,
and here the inspired writer tells us that when we defend
our faith, we are to do it _"with meekness and fear."_

We can't discuss matters of eternal life with an attitude
of arrogance or anger. These conversations should be
motivated by a genuine concern for the soul of another

and characterized by gentleness and humility. The "fear" we have is in regard to the gravity of the Gospel message and respect for its soul-saving capability, not fear born of uncertainty or weakness. When we approach others in kindness and in love and in reverence to God, we have a better chance that they will hear what we have to say!

How can you demonstrate *"meekness and fear"* when you speak to others on matter of faith, without compromising the Truth? _____

_____

_____

In Ephesians 4:15, we read that the truth should be spoken in love. Why is it important for love to be our motivation and attitude when it comes to sharing the Truth? _____

_____

4.   **Be available to be used by God**

Years ago, I remember sitting in a leadership class at a hospital and being given the assignment to "list the most important qualities of a leader." When everyone finished making their lists, we shared them with each other. I will never forget the first quality mentioned by one of the older nurses in the group: **availability**.

"Availability?" I thought. "What a strange quality to choose." However, as time has passed, I have come to appreciate *availability* as one of the most admirable of leadership qualities.

It is difficult to be influenced by someone who is never around; it is impossible to receive instruction from someone you cannot contact; and it is discouraging to try to maintain a relationship with someone who is always "too busy." In order to help, teach, and encourage others....you have to be **available**.

This is especially true when it comes to serving in God's kingdom. We have to be available to use the gifts He has given us in order to further the work of the church.

Huldah had a husband, she had a home, she may have had a family, and she may have had a career; but when she was needed to do God's work, she was ready!

God has shown time and time again in Scripture that He uses people, even when they may feel unprepared or unqualified. Just think of Moses, Rahab, Mary, the Apostles, and Paul to name only a few! He can do amazing things with our lives when we make ourselves available to Him.

Think of some other men and women in the Bible who accomplished extraordinary things because they made themselves available to God. _____

_____

_____

In what ways are you using your talents to serve God in the church? _____

_____

How can you make yourself more available to God? _____

_____

_____

"Here I am, send me!" Isaiah 6:8

◤TRAILMARKERS

1. Where do we find the account of Huldah in the Bible? _____

    _____

2. Who became the king of Judah after the evil reigns of
    Manasseh and Amon? _____

    _____

3. How old was he when he became king? _____

4. Was he a good king or a bad king? _____

    _____

5. Describe the Israelites relationship with God at this time. _

    _____

    _____

    _____

6. What did Josiah begin to do at the age of sixteen? _____

    _____

    _____

    _____

    _____

7. In the eighteenth year of Josiah's reign, what important
    work did he begin? _____

    _____

8. Who did he put in charge of this effort? _____

_____

9. What did Hilkiah, the high priest, find in the Temple? _____

_____

_____

10. What is that book commonly believed to have been? _____

_____

_____

11. Who read the contents of the book to the king? _____

_____

_____

12. What did Josiah do when after the Law was read to him? __

_____

_____

13. What important task did Josiah give to five of his men? __

_____

_____

14. To whom did Josiah's men go? _____

_____

15. What was the message that was communicated to Josiah?

_____

_____

_____

_____

16. What blessing would Josiah receive because of his
faithfulness? _____

_____

17. What was the direct result of Huldah's prophecy? _____

_____

_____

18. In what way was Huldah respected? _____

_____

_____

19. How did she prove herself ready for God? _____

_____

_____

_____

_____

20. What strength training tips do we learn from Huldah?

1.

2.

3.

4.

CHAPTER 13

THEIR LEGACY

LESSON TEXT /// THIS ONE IS UP TO YOU!

You've read the powerful accounts of eleven trailblazing women in the Old Testament and observed, through Scripture, their strength in action. Their stories may be often unsung, but details of their lives were recorded by divine inspiration for our learning and encouragement today. How you apply their strength-building characteristics in your own life and continue to walk the narrow path following their examples of faith is up to you!

◣TRAILHEAD

In this study you have met a woman who:

1. Was asked to do something morally wrong

2. Sought justice and changed the law

3. Was married to a foolish man

4. Inspired an oppressed nation

5. Encouraged a hesitant leader

6. Suffered because of someone else's mistake

7. Struggled with infertility

8. Had to deliver bad news to a good person

9. Defended a loved one who had been treated badly

10. Stood up to a powerful leader

11. Maintained peace in a volatile situation

12. Begged God in prayer for a blessing

13. Used the resources she had to help others and overcome evil

14. Gave up something she cherished

15. Made a quick judgment in a critical situation

16. Submitted to something she did not want because it was the right thing to do

17. Shared God's Word with someone needing guidance

18. Faced the death of someone she loved

On the surface, their incredible accounts may seem irrelevant to modern-day Christian women, but with a closer look we find that our Old Testament sisters faced the same trials and temptations that we do today. They dealt with issues that tested their faith, they weathered storms of life that tried their resolve, and they faced difficult situations that proved their character; but through their strength they overcame!

YOUR TRUE STORY

"GET READY"

The course has been set, the trail is well marked, and a prize awaits you at the finish! But first, there are a few important details to remember that will help you along the way. Before you begin... prepare to **W.A.L.K.**!

 Get ready to **W.A.L.K.**

> **W**ear Good Shoes – *Ephesians 6:15; Isaiah 52:7*
>
> **A**pply Son Screen – *Psalm 40:11; 2Thessalonians 3:3*
>
> **L**ighten Your Load – *Psalm 55:22; 1 Peter 5:7*
>
> **K**now Where You're Headed – *Philippians 3:14, 20-21; 2 Timothy 4:7-8*

WEAR GOOD SHOES

This is a must before you start walking! Good shoes will give support, provide comfort, maintain traction, and ensure stability— all of which work together to help prevent injury. For Christians, there is specific instruction given in the Bible as to what type of foot covering we should have in our daily walk:

"...and having shod your feet with the preparation of the gospel of peace" (Ephesians 6:15).

The Christian shoe is the Gospel! There is no better means of support, comfort, traction, stability, and injury prevention than the good news of Jesus Christ. As we follow the trail walked by our faithful sisters, we bring with us the message of salvation; it cushions us, protects us, carries us, and makes our feet beautiful!

"How beautiful upon the mountains are the feet of him who brings the good news, who proclaims peace, who brings glad tidings of good things, who proclaims salvation, who says to Zion, 'Your God reigns!'" (Isaiah 52:7).

Remember to wear good shoes!

APPLY SON SCREEN

In recent years, we've heard a great deal about the need to shield ourselves from the harmful rays of the sun. Much attention is given to our earthly bodies as we carefully lather on the SPF 30. We want to preserve our youthful skin for as long as possible.

But there is something even more important that is needed to protect us from the outside forces we encounter in our Christian walk! David wrote in Psalm 40: 11, *"Do not withhold Your tender mercies from me, O Lord; let Your loving-kindness and Your truth continually preserve me."*

Paul, by inspiration, told the Thessalonians, *"The Lord is faithful, who will establish you and guard you from the evil one"* (2 Thessalonians 3:3).

The love, truth, and faithfulness of Jesus Christ will preserve us and guard us through this life. We need to continually pray for His protection, apply His teachings to our lives daily, cover ourselves with His example, and defend ourselves against evil through His Word.

Check to be sure you have applied your Son screen!

LIGHTEN YOUR LOAD

You don't need anything weighing you down on this journey! In order to keep up your endurance and perform your best, you will have to remove the backpack of "wish-I-hadn'ts," "shoulda-beens," and "what-ifs." Sometimes we have a hard time letting go of that backpack. After all, we've invested a large amount of our time and energy into filling it up, but Jesus wants us to hand it over to Him so that He can help ease our suffering.

"Cast your burden on the Lord, and He shall sustain you; He shall never permit the righteous to be moved" (Psalm 55:22).

"Casting all your care upon Him, for He cares for you" (1 Peter 5:7).

Jesus doesn't want you to be burdened with guilt, regret, and worry as you walk the trail; give those things to the Savior who loves you, cares for you, and who has promised to take care of you every day.

Don't forget to lighten your load!

KNOW WHERE YOU'RE HEADED

Our trailblazing sisters of the Old Testament walked a path through Bible lands. They followed God-given signs, witnessed His miraculous power firsthand, and heard His words spoken directly through prophets. They trusted in God, they obeyed His commands, and they knew they were headed for a Land of Promise.

Through the Gospel plan of salvation we can continue to follow in the steps of those strong women and walk the trail that is identified on the pages of the New Testament.

Every trail has a destination. Do you know what trail you are on and where it is leading? Paul knew, and it gave him the encouragement he needed to keep going:

"I press toward the goal of the prize of the upward call of God in Christ Jesus" (Philippians 3:14).

As he neared the end of his life, Paul spoke again of the prize for which he had been striving:

"I have fought the good fight, I have finished the race, I have kept the faith. Finally, there is laid up for me the crown of righteousness, which the Lord, the righteous Judge, will give to me on that Day, and not to me only but also to all who have loved His appearing" (2 Timothy 4:7-8).

The Christian's trail is difficult and is accessed through a narrow gate, but for the faithful traveler, it will lead to a crown and an eternal home in Heaven. We are sure to stumble, we might even fall down flat, but we keep pressing toward the goal because of the reward we have been promised.

 God does not call us through the Gospel to be perfect; He calls us to be faithful.

"For our citizenship is in heaven, from which we also eagerly wait for the Savior, the Lord Jesus Christ, who will transform our lowly body that it may be conformed to His glorious body, according to the

working by which He is able even to subdue all things to Himself" (Philippians 3:20-21).

Always know where you are headed!

"GET SET"

As you grow in strength, find ways to use it! Look for opportunities to share your faith, to stand up for what is right, to help others, and to encourage peace. Rely on your strength for coping in hard times, for dealing with daily challenges, and for submitting to God's Will. Put your strength to work in the kingdom of God!

Here is what we can know from the Scripture: God values women. He loves them and blesses them with talents that can be used in His kingdom. Those talents are widely varied and might include teaching, writing, speaking, encouraging, cooking, crafting, leading, organizing, decorating, cleaning, or singing. Talents can also be related to athletics, technology, or academics. Whatever your ability, or abilities, there is a capacity in which to use your talent for the purpose of spreading Christianity in harmony with God's organization of the church. If you look for opportunities to serve, you will find them!

God has shown throughout time that He recognizes the worth of women:

· We are made in His image

· He chose a woman to bear His Son

· The mothers of the kings of Judah and Israel are consistently remembered by name in the Old Testament

- One of the best remembered prayers of the Bible was spoken by a woman who longed for a son (Who was she? _____ 1 Samuel 1:10-11)

- Among the most beautiful songs of praise found in Scripture were those sung by women

---

We've read the heartfelt songs of Deborah and Hannah in this study. Now, read the words of Mary, the mother of Jesus, in Luke 1:46-55, sung in praise to God for His marvelous blessing!

- Women were actively involved in Jesus' ministry

- The longest one-on-one conversation Jesus had, recorded in Scripture, was with a woman (Who was she? _____ John 4:1-42)

- Jesus repeatedly used women as examples of faith in the Old and New Testament

- Jesus was first seen by women following His resurrection

- Women helped to spread the Gospel of Jesus Christ after the establishment of the New Testament church

We can do so much good for the Lord! Strong women trust in God's plan to preserve His church throughout time and find ways to serve Him that are in keeping with the guidelines He has provided us in Scripture.

"GO!"

The church needs her members to be strong. The time is now and the need is urgent! Christians are going to face hard times; in fact, Paul tells us to expect it! He told Timothy in 2 Timothy 3:12 that *"all who desire to live godly in Christ Jesus will suffer persecution."*

When we face persecution...and we will, if we take a stand for the Word of God...we must be ready to fight for our faith and defend what we believe. But also, like Paul, we endure all things for the sake of the church, so that others *"may obtain the salvation which is in Christ Jesus with eternal glory"* (2 Timothy 2:10).

Our faith is going to be tested as our country faces a moral decline now more than ever before. Are we ready? Do we have the ability to overcome? Think of the confidence of Puah and Shiphrah, the pursuit of justice by Mahlah, Noah, Hoglah, Milcah, and Tirzah, the bravery of Deborah, the resourcefulness of Jael, the submissiveness of Jephthah's daughter, the patience of Hannah, the discernment of Abigail, the wisdom of the woman of Abel, the love of Rizpah, the kindness of the Shunammite woman, the readiness of Huldah... and allow the strength of these women to empower you and provide you with hope for the future.

Their legacy lives on!

STRENGTH TRAINING TIPS

1. **To be a woman of strength, you must train daily**

    Just as athletes train to improve their performance,

Christians must train to increase their strength. Wanting to be strong is an important first step, but then effort is required. In order to become stronger, we have to work!

Strength training for the Christian involves the two principles James wrote about in James 1:22-25, *"hearing"* and *"doing."* We have to **hear** the Word of God (to build up our faith – Romans 10:17) and then we have to **do** what it says (to perfect, or complete, our faith – James 2:22). James described a working faith—a faith that exercises; and the Christian who exercises her faith daily is the Christian who increases her strength daily.

We can remember the example of the Bereans in Acts 17:11 (emp. added) in that *"they received the word with all readiness and **searched the Scriptures daily** to find out whether these things were so."*

Knowing that *"faith comes by hearing and hearing by the Word of God"* (Romans 10:17)…imagine how our faith would grow if we commit ourselves to daily searching the Scriptures!

Reading the Bible helps us come to know God: His Will for our lives, His plan to save us by His grace, and His immeasurable love for mankind. It is within the pages of the Bible that we discover what we must do to accept His gift of grace and how to live the life of a Christian. The Bible, breathed from the mouth of God, is our faith source. It is where we find our belief, our hope, and our call to action!

But it is not enough to simply *hear* the Word of God, we must follow through…and *do*! We can read every book on fitness that has ever been written and know exactly what we need to do to gain physical strength, but our condition will not improve without putting that knowledge into practice. The same is true with our faith! We can read the Bible and know exactly what we need to do in order to become a stronger Christian, but without doing the work, our condition will not improve.

Doing what the Bible says means obeying the commands that have been given to us by God. This is how we fully come to know Him (1 John 2:3-6) and how we demonstrate our love for Him (John 14:15). Our obedience should originate from a sincere and humble spirit that longs to serve God, no matter what the cost.

When we *hear* and *do* the Will of God every day, we exercise our faith and our strength will grow.

How do you plan to exercise your faith daily so that you can become a stronger Christian? _____

_____

_____

2. **Be certain that you are on the right trail**

Paul wrote in Ephesians 4:4-6, *"There is one body and one Spirit, just as you were called in one hope of your calling; one Lord, one faith, one baptism; one God and Father of all, who is above all, and through all, and in you all."*

There are many trails we can choose to walk in this life, but there is only one trail that will take us to Heaven. It is accessed through a narrow gate, it promises to be difficult at times, only a few will find it, but it is the trail that leads to eternal life (Matthew 7:13-14).

In John 14:6, Jesus said, *"I am the way, the truth, and the life. No one comes to the Father except through me."*

Jesus also said in John 10:9, *"I am the door. If anyone enters by Me, he will be saved, and will go in and out and find pasture."*

The world offers other trails that are much easier to walk and some that lead to short-lived happiness, but the trail that is accessed through Christ is the trail that will bring joy and everlasting reward. It is not a secret trail; it is clearly identified in the New Testament, and can be found through reading the Word of God.

With the Bible as our trail guide, we enter the gate by obedience to God's plan for our salvation through the gracious gift of His Son, and then we walk faithfully along the trail, conducting ourselves in a manner that is *"worthy of the gospel of Christ"* (Philippians 1:27, Ephesians 4:1). In other words, we live a life that is consistent with God's Word—which will not always be easy, but with help and hope we can get through the difficult times!

We have the help of our Heavenly Father who will never leave us or forsake us (Deuteronomy 31:8); the help of the Holy Spirit in prayer and through the Word (Romans 8:26, John 14:16-17); and the help of our brothers and sisters in Christ who will encourage us and lift us up when we fall (1 Thessalonians 5:11). We also have the hope that has been laid up for us in Heaven (Colossians 1:5) and the hope of eternal life which God has promised (1 John 2:25) if we remain faithful.

Read Matthew 7:13-14. The broad way is not marked by Satan with signs that say: "This is the way to destruction ⟫⟫." It is a way of deception that seems right and is chosen by many, but Proverbs 14:12 and Proverbs 16:25 tell us that *"its end is the way of death."*

Why do so many people choose to follow the "broad" way?

_____

_____

Why is the right way referred to as the "difficult" way? ____

_____

_____

How can you be sure you are on the trail that leads to eternal life? _____

_____

3. **Be joyful on your journey**

There is no better life than the life of a Christian!

"The Lord has done great things for us and we are glad" (Psalm 126:3).

God has blessed us abundantly. The Bible tells us that *"every good and perfect gift is from above"* (James 1:17), and our lives are filled with evidences of God's love and generosity. When I think of my husband, my children, my parents, my sisters and their families, all of my extended family and the family I gained when I married Sam, my church family, my home—I am overwhelmed with the gifts God has placed in my life. What would my life be without them? I simply cannot imagine.

But in as much as God has enriched our lives with physical blessings, He has given us something even greater! He has given us the best, most complete gift—a gift that is so marvelous that it is "unspeakable" (2 Corinthians 9:15)—the gift of His Son, Jesus Christ in whom He has *"blessed us with every spiritual blessing in the heavenly places"* (Ephesians 1:3).

In Ephesians 1:4-14 Paul explained what those spiritual blessings are for the Christian:

God chose us before the foundation of the world that we should be holy and blameless, He adopted us as His children through Jesus Christ, He offered us the riches of His grace by which we are redeemed and forgiven of our sins, He made known to us the Gospel, He has given us an eternal inheritance, and He has sealed us with the Holy Spirit of promise.

We should be filled with joy on our journey through this life because of the immeasurable blessings we have in Christ.

List some of the blessings you have received that bring you joy in this journey. _____

_____

4. **Write your own true story of strength that can be shared with future generations**

As author, you hold the pen and write the sentences that create your life story. What will it tell? Is it a story of hope, or of happiness? Is it a story of love?

Whatever the theme may be, let me encourage you to also make it a story of strength. Be the heroine with character and conviction, capable of withstanding evil forces, and not easily captured or defeated. Be the Christian woman who, by a whispering strength or a thundering strength, influences the world around her every day.

Write a life story that will inspire others to be strong! Live faithfully, always looking for ways to serve God and never compromising the Truth. By following in the footsteps of the trailblazing women we have studied, you not only continue their legacy of strength…you also create your own!

If your children, and your children's children, were able to read your life story, what message would you want them to glean from its pages? _____

_____

_____

What title would you want written on the cover of your story? _____

_____

Reflect on the words of this poem when you consider the story of your life and the theme that is revealed within its pages:

AS THE YEARS GO BY

Her life is a precious story, written by her very hand,
Each step she takes becomes a word, according to the Father's plan.

As a child, He gave to her a pen, unseen to human eye
And a book of empty pages to be filled as time passed by.

Many chapters she has authored now from a life lived long and true
There's adventure, there is love, but there is pain and sorrow, too.

Her story is one of faith, trusting in God when hard times come,
Standing strong against the world when easier to succumb.

It's also a story of patience, of happiness, of fears,
It's a tale that's marked with laughter, marked with smiles,
marked with tears.

Everyone who reads her finds a book of inspiring hope,
Her words teach perseverance and strength that is needed to cope:

With certainty she writes her steps; she does not simply roam,
As the years go by, her theme is clear: life is a going home.

by Lori Boyd

 "I can do all things through Christ who strengthens me."
Philippians 4:13

◣ TRAILMARKERS

1. Under the Trailhead section of this chapter, name each woman referred to in numbers 1 through 17? (Write their names next to their description. Some names will be used more than once).

2. What does the mnemonic W.A.L.K. stand for, as discussed in this chapter?

    W =

    A =

    L =

    K =

3. In Ephesians 6:15, what does the Bible say should cover the feet of a Christian? _____

    _____

4. In Isaiah 52:7, whose feet are described as beautiful? ____

    _____

5. According to that same verse, what is the Gospel and what does it proclaim? _____

    _____

    _____

    _____

6. What will guard us and preserve us in this life? _____

    _____

    _____

    _____

7. How can we seek the protection of Jesus? _____

_____

_____

_____

8. What emotions can cause us to feel burdened along the
trail? _____

_____

_____

9. How can we "lighten our load" in our daily Christian walk?

_____

_____

10. How can we identify the trail we are to follow as
Christians? _____

_____

11. Where does that trail lead? _____

_____

12. What did Paul say was "laid up for him" after finishing the
race and keeping the faith? _____

_____

13. In what ways can your strength be used to work in the
kingdom of God? _____

_____

_____

14. How can a woman's leadership talents be used in the
church and remain in harmony with the Scripture? _____

_____

_____

15. In whose image was woman created? _____

16. List three examples from the Bible that demonstrate the value of women. _____

_____

_____

_____

17. What did Paul tell Timothy in 2 Timothy 3:12 about those who desire to live godly in Christ Jesus? _____

_____

_____

18. What reason did Paul give Timothy as to why we endure all things for the sake of the church? _____

_____

_____

19. As this study comes to a close, which trailblazing sister's account has left the greatest impression on you, and why?

_____

_____

_____

20. We have discussed twenty-two characteristics of eleven different trailblazing women of the Old Testament. Which of those characteristics do you think are the most important for the strong Christian woman to possess? ____

_____

_____

_____

_____

Made in the USA
San Bernardino, CA
16 February 2016